DEC 00

Remarkable Women: Past and Present

Reformers

Reformers

Activists, Educators, Religious Leaders

Monique Avakian

RAINTREE
STECK-VAUGHN
PUBLISHERS

A Harcourt Company

Austin · New York
www.steck-vaughn.com

Published by Raintree Steck-Vaughn Publishers, an imprint of Steck-Vaughn Company

CREATED IN ASSOCIATION WITH MEDIA PROJECTS INCORPORATED
C. Carter Smith, *Executive Editor*
Carter Smith III, *Managing Editor*
Monique Avakian, *Principal Writer*
Ana Deboo, *Project Editor*
Bernard Schleifer, *Art Director*
John Kern, *Cover Design*
Karen Covington, *Production Editor*

RAINTREE STECK-VAUGHN PUBLISHERS STAFF
Walter Kossmann, *Publishing Director*
Kathy DeVico, *Editor*
Richard Dooley, *Design Project Manager*

Photos on front cover, clockwise from top left: Gloria Steinem, Princess Diana, Harriet Tubman, Dolores Huerta

Photos on cover page, top to bottom: Susan B. Anthony, Dorothy Height, Rosa Luxemburg, Mother Teresa

Acknowledgments listed on page 80 constitute part of this copyright page.

Library of Congress Cataloging-in-Publication Data
Avakian, Monique.
    Reformers: activists, educators, religious leaders / Monique Avakian.
        p.   cm. — (Remarkable women: past and present)
    Includes index.
    Summary: Brief biographies of notable women who have contributed significantly to the fields of education, political activism, and religion, from Halide Edib Adivar to Victoria Claflin Woodhull.
        ISBN 0-8172-5733-0
        1. Women social reformers—Biography. 2. Women political activists—Biography. 3. Women educators—Biography. 4. Women and religion—Biography. [1. Educators. 2. Women in religion. 3. Reformers. 4. Women—Biography.] I. Title. II. Series: Remarkable women.
HQ1123.A93   2000
305.4'092'2—dc21   98-54841
                                                                            CIP AC

Printed and bound in the United States
1 2 3 4 5 6 7 8 9 0 LB 03 02 01 00 99

CONTENTS

INTRODUCTION

IN THIS BOOK YOU'LL FIND PROFILES OF A WIDE VARIETY OF WOMEN reformers from all over the world. It may surprise you to learn that in Rome over 2,000 years ago, a woman named Hortensia stormed into a government meeting and demanded a fairer taxation policy—successfully. Or that in Japan, where women were not allowed to vote until 1946, the American suffrage movement had a strong, inspiring effect on such women as Ichikawa Fusae and Hiratsuka Raicho.

You will read about many different ways of protesting or sparking change. Elizabeth Cady Stanton and Susan B. Anthony, the most famous American reformers, established associations, organized conferences, led protests, and gave speeches. Some, like Barbara Bodichon, established schools for women. Jane Addams set up "settlement houses" where social workers and the needy could live and work together. Olympe de Gouges wrote an eloquent criticism of women's treatment in revolutionary France. Some activists, like the Pankhursts and Rosa Luxemburg, concluded that they could only draw attention to their cause through violence. Harriet Tubman threw herself bodily into the abolitionist cause, risking her life dozens of times to save others. Mother Teresa tended to the most basic emotional and physical needs of the suffering poor in Calcutta, India.

One quality all these women have in common, and in abundance, is optimism. They just can't believe it isn't possible to change whatever is wrong—even if it sometimes seems they are trying to move mountains. They persevere: the 19th Amendment finally granted American women the right to vote. Victory! Did Maud Wood Park relax? No, she immediately formed the League of Women Voters so she could help women learn *how* to use that hard-won vote intelligently. In Pauli Murray's quest for an ever-more advanced education, she applied to universities that rejected her because she was African American or because she was a woman. Never mind. If one school refused her, Murray went to another, and more often than not, she also took steps to change the unfair admissions policies that had stood in her way.

That's not to say they are all saints (although a few of them *are*). Women are people, too, after all. Winnie Mandela, after years of good work fighting apartheid, let her power go to her head and committed crimes. In the 1860s the American suffragists grew so embroiled in squabbles that they divided into rival camps and made little progress for years. It's important to know these things, because we can learn from other people's mistakes. We can see how important it is to work together, to plan strategies carefully, and to know when to work within established systems and when to break free and demand new policies.

Another thing: All these women (and others, too) did far more than we can possibly mention in our limited space. So when somebody interests you, do a little more research. See what else she accomplished. Read something she wrote or a book about her. Maybe her cause is one you agree with and can get involved in. Because there's still plenty to be done.

Photos top left Emmeline Pankhurst, bottom left Maria Montessori, top right Ella Baker, bottom right Maude Gonne.

Joy Adamson (1910–1980)
Conservationist, painter, writer

JOY ADAMSON HELPED TO BRING WILDLIFE conservation to world attention. Her book, *Born Free* (1960), later made into a popular movie, tells the story of how she raised a lion cub, Elsa, and released her into the wild. Her relationships with Elsa's cubs are detailed in *Living Free* (1961) and *Forever Free* (1962). She also wrote about her work with a cheetah she named Pippa.

Born in Austria, Adamson grew up far from the African wilds and took some time to discover her calling. She considered a number of careers—including concert pianist, archaeologist, and physician—before she discovered her love of wildlife during a trip to Kenya in 1937. She married George Adamson, a British chief game warden who was posted in Africa, in 1943. During the 1950s she was able to put her considerable talent as a painter and photographer to use on a project to document vanishing tribal life. The artworks she produced during that time, over 600 of them, belong to the permanent collection of the National Museum of Kenya.

In 1980 Adamson was killed. Rumors circulated that she had been mauled by a lion, but eventually a man was arrested and accused of the murder. Her legacy to animal conservation continues today with the World Wildlife Fund, which Adamson founded in 1962.

Jane Addams (1860–1935)
Social reformer, pacifist

JANE ADDAMS WENT TO ROCKFORD COLLEGE, NOT far from her hometown of Cedarville, Illinois, and received her degree in 1881. Originally she wanted to become a doctor, so she enrolled at the Woman's Medical College of Pennsylvania. But poor health forced her to leave her studies. Then, in 1889, she traveled to London with her friend Ellen Gates Starr. At the Toynbee Hall settlement there, she found a different way to help people. The idea of the "settlement" movement was that people helping the poor should live in the same neighborhoods and work to create classless communities.

The next year, Addams and Starr founded Hull House in a run-down section of Chicago. Anyone was welcome to go there for help and inspiration. They could learn new trade skills, receive medical care, and put on plays and concerts. Immigrants came to learn English. The people who worked there—mainly women—received training as social workers. By 1910, when Addams published her famous book, *Twenty Years at Hull-House*, similar settlement houses had opened all across America.

Addams worked with many other reform groups outside of Hull House. Not everyone liked her politics. Some wealthy people did not think, as Addams did, that workers should form trade unions. When Addams supported the unions, they stopped making contributions to Hull House. However, she remained true to her beliefs. She continued to fight for women's suffrage, free speech, and workers' rights.

Motivated by the outbreak of World War I in 1914, Addams devoted herself to the pacifist movement. In 1931, four years before her death, she was one of two winners of the Nobel Peace Prize.

> "A city is in many respects a great business corporation, but in other respects it is enlarged housekeeping. . . . May we not say that city housekeeping has failed partly because women, the traditional housekeepers, have not been consulted as to its multiform activities?"
>
> JANE ADDAMS
> "Utilization of Women in City Government," 1907

Halide Edib Adivar (1884–1964)

Feminist, activist, novelist

HALIDE EDIB ADIVAR LIVED DURING A TIME OF dramatic cultural and political change in Turkey, and her childhood fittingly mirrored her country's situation. Her father, a government official for the Sultan Abdül-hamid II, raised and educated her in the English manner. Her grandmother taught her folk medicine and conservative Muslim traditions.

Throughout her life, Adivar worked for educational reform, women's rights, and Turkish independence. She was a prolific writer, producing essays, stories, plays, and over 20 novels. The women in her fiction were rebels, who fought oppression and worked to educate their people as she did.

Following World War I, Adivar joined the nationalist rebels led by Mustafa Kemal Atatürk in their fight for Turkish independence. Atatürk did become the new republic's first president, but he grew increasingly ruthless and authoritarian. Adivar and her husband, like many liberals who had supported independence, were forced into exile. Living abroad after 1924, she wrote her auto-biography—an almost unheard-of project for a Middle Eastern woman—and lectured at American universities. After Atatürk's death in 1938, she returned home, where she taught at the university in Istanbul and, from 1950 to 1954, served in the Turkish parliament.

Elizabeth Cabot Cary Agassiz (1822–1907)

Educator, writer

ALTHOUGH ELIZABETH AGASSIZ RECEIVED HER OWN education at her family home in Boston, she went on to promote the idea of formal educational institutions for women. In the early part of her life, however, she devoted herself to helping her husband, the famous Swiss naturalist and Harvard professor, Louis Agassiz.

It was not that Elizabeth sacrificed her own intellectual life in favor of her husband's. They often worked as a team. Many of Louis's scientific papers are based on her notes. She helped him plan his travels and frequently went with him. After visiting Brazil with the Thayer Expedition in 1865, they coauthored *A Journey in Brazil* (1867). In 1871 they joined the Hassler Expedition on its way through the Strait of Magellan. Returning home, they opened a summer school and marine laboratory. Elizabeth also published several books of her own.

After Louis's death in 1873, Elizabeth wrote his biography. Then she joined a handful of people interested in opening a women's college where the teachers would be Harvard professors. The institution was at first called the "Harvard Annex." In 1894 the Annex became officially affiliated with Harvard, and it was renamed in honor of Ann Radcliffe, a 17th-century philanthropist who had provided funds for the first Harvard scholarship. Elizabeth Agassiz served as the president of the school from 1882 to 1899, and stayed on as honorary president until 1903.

Susan Brownell Anthony (1820–1906)

Suffragist, social reformer

SUSAN B. ANTHONY'S CAREER AS A SOCIAL REFORMER started when, as a schoolteacher in rural New York, she fought for equal pay for male and female teachers. She went on to join the temperance movement. Then in 1852, Anthony attended a Sons of Temperance meeting with Elizabeth Cady Stanton and other female reformers. All of the women who were there were forbidden to speak. Angered at this injustice on the part of men claiming to be progressives, Anthony and Stanton began their life-long partnership in the fight for women's rights.

After the Civil War ended, the two women established *The Revolution*, a newspaper dedicated to supporting women's suffrage. Some reformers wanted suffragists to keep a back seat until black men got the vote. But Anthony and Stanton, who had both supported abolition, refused to wait. They formed the National Woman Suffrage Association (NWSA) in 1869. Their goal was to amend the Constitution to allow women to vote. Other suffragists joined the American Woman Suffrage Association (AWSA), which worked for suffrage at the state level.

At the 1872 presidential election, Anthony led a group of women in casting their votes. Arrested and fined, she refused to pay. Instead, she wrote a report about her experience. She argued that nothing in the Constitution specifically stated that women were not allowed to vote.

In 1890 the NWSA and AWSA united to form the National American Woman Suffrage Association, and Anthony served as president from 1892 to 1900. After that she continued to write and lecture. Anthony died before her dream of women's suffrage became a reality. However, she never gave up hope. In her final speech, delivered in Baltimore in 1906, she predicted, "Failure is impossible!"

Anne Askew (1521–1546)
Protestant martyr

A NNE ASKEW LIVED IN ENGLAND DURING THE reign of King Henry VIII, a time when Roman Catholics and Protestants (also known then as Reformers) were deadly enemies. Trapped in an unhappy marriage, she may have moved to London hoping to get a divorce. Once there, she joined a group of Protestants and attracted the attention of powerful Catholic church officials who arrested her for heresy in 1545.

The details of Askew's trial are known because a Protestant named John Bale published her writings after her death. Askew presented events in dialogue form, and her words show that she was very clever. She made a point of tricking the authorities into debating religious issues by answering their questions with questions of her own. This outraged them because women were forbidden even to read the Bible in public, let alone discuss it. They tried to force her to reveal the names of other "heretics." When Askew refused, she was tortured. Finally in July of 1546, Askew was sentenced to death and burned at the stake, immediately becoming a martyr to her faith.

Sarah Bagley (1806–after 1848)
Labor reformer, journalist

W HEN SARAH BAGLEY LEFT HER FAMILY'S New Hampshire farm in 1837, she looked forward to working at the textile mills in Lowell, Massachusetts. Back then the "City of Spindles," as Lowell was called, promised broadened horizons and better educational opportunities. The attraction soon passed, however, as Bagley struggled through workdays lasting 12 hours or more, wage cuts, increasing machine "speedups," and suffered health problems caused by the poor factory air.

Bagley decided to fight. She founded Lowell's Female Labor Reform Association in 1844, and it sprouted chapters throughout New England. Her goals were to get the State government to inspect the mills and to reduce the workday to ten hours. She joined other labor groups as well, including the New England Working Men's Association, whose paper, *The Voice of Industry*, she helped write and edit.

In spite of all Bagley's work, the so-called Ten Hour Movement was dead by 1848, and the Massachusetts legislature did not respond to her demands. After a stint as the nation's first female telegraph operator, Bagley is documented as having returned briefly to mill work. Then she left Lowell. No further details are known about her.

Ella Baker (1903–1986)
Civil rights activist, organizer

E LLA BAKER PLAYED A KEY ROLE in the 20th-century Civil Rights movement, participating in nearly every organization dedicated to her cause. Born in North Carolina, she graduated from Shaw University and moved to Harlem in New York City. During the 1930s and 1940s, she worked for the Young Negro Cooperative League, the Work Projects Administration, and the NAACP.

In the early 1950s, Baker moved to Alabama to lend her

experience and organizing expertise to the fledgling Civil Rights movement. She advised Dr. Martin Luther King, Jr. during the Montgomery bus boycott and helped found the Southern Christian Leadership Conference. Baker acted as mentor to students across the South as they planned sit-in protests, and she fostered the formation of the Student Nonviolent Coordinating Committee in 1960. Her lifelong dedication and unassuming but powerful skills inspired generations to action, dramatically altering the course of American history.

Emily Greene Balch (1867–1961)
Pacifist, social reformer, scholar

EMILY GREENE BALCH WAS AN EXTRAORDINARILY conscientious person who tried to use the advantages she had been given to benefit others. Her parents provided her with an education that was exceptional by any standard: After earning her degree at Bryn Mawr, Balch studied at the Sorbonne in Paris, the Harvard Annex, the University of Chicago, and the University of Berlin. And even when she was busy studying, she did welfare work, too. In 1896 she began teaching political economy at Wellesley College.

While at Wellesley, Balch became involved in labor reform and cofounded the Boston Women's Trade Union League. Increasingly convinced that factories, land, and industry should be under public ownership, she became a Socialist in 1906. The Communist scare that accompanied the outbreak of World War I cost her

the teaching job. At the same time, the war brought her to the primary political focus of her life—pacifism.

Balch supported a variety of pacifist groups, including those headed by Jane Addams and Crystal Eastman. She cofounded the Women's International League for Peace and Freedom with Addams in 1919. In 1921, renouncing socialism, she became a Quaker. Balch regarded America's entry into World War II as an unfortunate necessity for defeating Hitler, but she did not support American nationalism. Instead she fought for the welfare of Japanese-Americans in U.S. prison camps and of Jewish refugees from Germany. For her work, Balch won the Nobel Peace Prize in 1946.

Toni Cade Bambara (1939–1995)
Civil rights activist, writer, teacher

TONI CADE FOUND THE NAME BAMBARA IN A sketchbook that had belonged to her great-grandmother, and it so appealed to her that she adopted it legally in 1970. Establishing that kind of a link with the past was in keeping with her work. Through her writings and social service, Bambara celebrated black culture and community.

In 1962 Bambara started graduate school in literature at City College in New York. At the same time, she coordinated neighborhood programs for veterans, the illiterate, and the mentally ill. She became involved in civil rights and women's rights. Bambara also began writing short stories, which were later collected in *Gorilla, My Love* (1972).

As an editor, Bambara planned the groundbreaking anthology *The Black Woman* (1970). In order to convey black women's thoughts about the civil and

> "Revolution begins with the self, in the self. The individual, the basic revolutionary unit, must be purged of poison and lies that assault the ego and threaten the heart, that hazard the next larger unit—the couple or pair, that jeopardize the still larger unit—the family or cell, that put the entire movement in peril."
>
> TONI CADE BAMBARA
> Lecture at Livingston College,
> Rutgers University, 1969

women's rights movements, she chose works by female students from City College, as well as by published writers like Alice Walker and Toni Morrison. The next year she edited *Tales and Stories for Black Folks* (1971) to encourage African Americans to learn more about their culture.

During the last half of the 1970s, Bambara traveled to Cuba and Vietnam and was writer-in-residence at Spelman College for three years. Then she settled in Philadelphia, where she wrote, taught, and worked with community groups until her death.

Clarissa Harlowe ("Clara") Barton (1821–1912)
Humanitarian, relief worker

CLARA BARTON DISCOVERED HER LIFE'S CALLING at age 11, when her older brother, David, fell from the roof of their barn in North Oxford, Massachusetts. He was badly hurt; Clara nursed him for two years until his health was restored. As it turned out, she would dedicate her whole life to caring for others.

During the Civil War, Barton decided to look after the desperately needy Union soldiers. She tended the wounded right on the battlefield, ignoring the bullets flying around her. The army doctors and soldiers

Wartime Humanitarianism

The First Geneva Convention was initiated by Henri Dunant, founder of the Red Cross, in 1864. His goal was to establish ground rules for wartime, so that wounded soldiers—from either side of the conflict—and the people caring for them were protected. When Clara Barton joined the Red Cross, most European governments had signed the agreement, but not the United States. Barton campaigned strenuously to convince her government of the importance of the idea. In 1882 she succeeded. There have since been additional Geneva Conventions, to clarify and broaden the terms of the accord. For example, in 1929 standards were set for the treatment of prisoners of war.

called the five-foot (1.5-m) tall volunteer the "Angel of the Battlefield." Barton worked so hard that her health failed, so in 1869 she went to Switzerland to recuperate. Instead of resting, she joined the International Red Cross and nursed soldiers behind German lines during the Franco-Prussian War of 1870.

When Barton returned home, she told Americans about the Red Cross, but since their country was not at war, few listened. She got their attention, though, when she argued that droughts, floods, hurricanes, and accidents produced victims, too. After years of campaigning, Barton established the American Red Cross in 1881. Barton was president of the American Red Cross for 23 years. Always a beloved figure in America, she continued to make public appearances until the end of her life.

Lady Margaret Beaufort (1443–1509)
Educator, founder of colleges

MARGARET BEAUFORT, BORN INTO A POWERFUL English family, married for the first time when she was 12—not an uncommon age in medieval times. Two years later, her husband, Edward Tudor, died, leaving her with a son. A second husband, Sir Henry Stafford, also died. Then, around 1473, she married Thomas, Lord Stanley, who helped her son win the famous Battle of Bosworth Field in 1485 and become King Henry VII of England. This marked the end of the civil conflicts known as the Wars of the Roses and the start of the Tudor dynasty.

At last, after years of struggle, Lady Margaret could retire from politics. Increasingly religious, she took monastic vows in 1504. However, instead of withdrawing to an isolated convent, she devoted herself to scholarly and charitable causes. She became a patron of the first English printing press operators, William Caxton and Wynkyn de Worde. Her greatest acts of generosity benefited Cambridge University; she founded Christ's College there in 1505 and left almost all her money to charter St. John's College after her death.

Catharine Esther Beecher (1800–1878)

Women's education supporter, anti-feminist

CATHARINE BEECHER BELONGED TO AN EXTREMELY influential American family. Her father, Lyman Beecher, and her brother, Henry Ward Beecher, were renowned ministers and social reformers. Her sister Harriet Beecher Stowe wrote the abolitionist novel *Uncle Tom's Cabin*. Catharine made her mark as an educator and with her efforts to affirm women's traditional social role.

Unlike her brother, Henry, Catherine did not support women's suffrage. She felt women should stay removed from politics. However, she did believe they should be able to support themselves. That conviction led her to promote educating women, especially to become teachers. Although most teachers were men, Beecher's argument was that women were natural moral leaders, better able to sacrifice themselves for others—ideal qualities in a teacher. With her sister Mary, she founded the Hartford Female Seminary in 1823. Leaving the school in 1831, she continued her work in Ohio and Wisconsin, as well as in the East.

At the same time, she promoted her ideas about women's role in society. In 1841 she published her most popular work, *A Treatise on Domestic Economy*, providing practical advice about domestic chores and efficiency in the home. She and her sister Harriet revised it together in 1869 and released it as *The American Woman's Home*, again to great success.

Annie Wood Besant (1847–1933)

Birth control activist, social reformer, Theosophist

ANNIE BESANT, A COMPELLING PUBLIC SPEAKER and tireless activist, had an unusual and controversial career. In 1873, newly separated from her husband, Besant became active with a group of radical London atheists led by Charles Bradlaugh. Among other causes, Besant and Bradlaugh supported teaching birth control to women. Their pamphlet about the subject led to their arrest on obscenity charges. In their defense, Besant spoke eloquently of the physical burden of multiple pregnancies on women and of the need for population control. Eventually they were declared innocent, but as a result of the scandal, Besant lost custody of her daughter, Mabel, to her husband.

Besant then turned to labor reform and joined a prominent group of socialists known as the Fabians. In 1888 she led a successful strike to improve the dangerous working conditions for "match girls," who worked in the match factories of London. She also helped to secure medical services and meal programs in schools.

Besant shocked many of her supporters by becoming a Theosophist in 1889. This spiritual movement, led by Helena Blavatsky, had Eastern and mystic overtones, and it seemed like the last thing to interest an atheist and socialist like Besant. Nevertheless, she remained with the Theosophists for the rest of her life. Named president of the group in 1907, she moved to India. There, in addition to spiritual work, she helped expand India's educational system and worked to promote the idea of home rule.

Mary McLeod Bethune (1875–1955)

Educator, civil rights activist, presidential adviser

MARY MCLEOD BETHUNE HAD TO FIGHT TO GET her education at a time when African Americans were not encouraged to go to school. Her parents, former slaves, could barely support their 17 children. But they encouraged Mary, and she won

scholarships to finance her education. She was the only black student at the Moody Bible Institute in Chicago when she graduated in 1895.

In 1904 Bethune moved to Daytona, Florida. There were no schools for young black women in town, and she planned to start one. But her life savings amounted to only $1.50, so she sold pies and solicited donations from churches to pay for her project: the Daytona Normal and Industrial Institute. At first her students sat at desks made of boxes, but the situation improved. In 1929 the college merged with an all-black men's school to become Bethune-Cookman College.

Bethune went on to work on a larger scale. She served as president of the National Association of Colored Women from 1924 to 1928. She helped form the National Council of Negro Women in 1935. Their mission was to improve the social and political standing of black women in America and abroad. Under President Franklin D. Roosevelt, Bethune became a member of the "Black Cabinet." This group of African American government officials advised the president on racial issues and worked to promote New Deal programs. She was also appointed director of the Federal Council on Negro Affairs.

Bethune won many awards for her work. Even after she retired from government service, she remained politically active in her home community in Daytona until her death.

Mary Ann Ball Bickerdyke (1817–1901)
Hospital worker, veterans' advocate

MOTHER BICKERDYKE CLAIMED A POSITION IN THE Union Army by seeing a job that needed to be done and doing it. A native of Ohio, Bickerdyke was a widow living in Illinois when the Civil War began in 1861. One day she volunteered to take supplies to an army hospital and was shocked by the unsafe conditions there.

Without even waiting to obtain permission, Bickerdyke set to work cleaning everything in sight, cooking up batches of food, and tending the wounded. The following year she was named an "agent in the field" for the Northwestern Sanitary Commission.

All through the war, the energetic Bickerdyke performed miracles of organization. She rescued wounded men from the battlefield, scavenged supplies, established laundries, and acted as a surgical assistant. She earned the love of the soldiers, the friendship of generals, and attention from the press. Taking advantage of her considerable influence with the generals Ulysses Grant and William Sherman, she had incompetent medical officers dismissed—and severely scolded them herself.

After the war, Bickerdyke continued to help the needy, collaborating with such organizations as the Salvation Army. She worked tirelessly for veterans, just as she had for active soldiers, lobbying Washington on their behalf.

Alice Stone Blackwell (1857–1950)
Suffragist, journalist

IT'S NO WONDER THAT ALICE BLACKWELL BECAME A leader in the suffrage movement. Her mother, Lucy Stone, was a cofounder of the American Woman Suffrage Association whose work was fully supported by her activist husband, Henry Browne Blackwell. Alice also had two accomplished aunts, the minister Antoinette Blackwell and the physician Elizabeth Blackwell.

Blackwell grew up in Orange, New Jersey, and Dorchester, Massachusetts. After graduating from Boston University in 1881, she started working for her mother as a writer and editor at the AWSA's *Woman's Journal*. It wasn't long before she had

assumed full control of the paper. She helped nudge the stalled women's suffrage movement forward by encouraging her mother to settle her differences with Susan B. Anthony. After Stone and Anthony merged their two organizations into the National American Woman Suffrage Association in 1890, Blackwell served as the group's recording secretary.

As passage of the 19th Amendment became a certainty, Blackwell retired from her job at the *Journal*, but not from politics. A founder of the Massachusetts League of Women Voters, she campaigned for the Progressive party during the 1924 elections. She also continued to write, translating poetry from several languages and publishing her mother's biography, *Lucy Stone: Pioneer in Woman's Rights*, in 1930.

Antoinette Louisa Brown Blackwell (1825–1921)
Ordained minister, social reformer, writer

AT NINE YEARS OLD, ANTOINETTE BROWN WAS SO sure of her religious calling that she made a public confession and became a full member of her Congregational Church. Even in her religious family, she was young for such a commitment.

Her faith remained strong, and while she was at Oberlin College in 1847, Antoinette chose to study theology. There was just one problem: it was unheard-of for a woman to become a minister in the 1800s. Her professors allowed her to attend classes, but they refused to let her graduate. She preached wherever she could anyway.

Then in 1853, the Congregational Church in South Butler, New York, offered her a job. This made her the first ordained woman pastor in America. Within a year, however, she discovered that her progressive beliefs clashed with the conservative ideas of her congregation. So she resigned and turned her attention to social reform issues such as temperance, suffrage, and abolition.

In 1856 Antoinette married Samuel C. Blackwell, Lucy Stone's brother. The couple had seven children, which limited Blackwell's public appearances. Instead she continued her influential reform work through the written word, producing nonfiction, fiction, and poetry. Blackwell also joined the American Woman Suffrage Association and lived long enough to cast a legal vote in 1920.

Harriot Eaton Stanton Blatch (1856–1940)
Suffragist

ELIZABETH CADY STANTON'S DAUGHTER, HARRIOT, married the British businessman William Blatch in 1882 and lived for two decades in England. After she returned to New York City in 1902, she gave the stalled American suffrage movement a much-needed boost. Always a bridge-builder, Blatch's contribution to her mother and Susan B. Anthony's *History of Woman Suffrage* (1881–1922) helped ease tensions between the rivals, AWSA and NWSA. In 1907, inspired by the success of headline-grabbers like the Englishwoman Emmeline Pankhurst, Blatch founded the Equality League of Self-Supporting Women. They held rallies and organized the first suffragist parades. She also led the campaign to promote a state suffrage amendment, forming political "pressure groups" and appearing annually before Albany's legislators from 1910 until 1917, when the law passed.

In 1913 Blatch joined forces with Alice Paul to campaign for a federal suffrage amendment. Unlike Paul, Blatch suspended her suffrage activities during World War I to support the war effort, and by the time peace was reestablished, the 19th Amendment had passed. Without pausing, Blatch turned to the next pressing issue, helping Paul to campaign for a federal Equal Rights Amendment.

Amelia Jenks Bloomer (1818–1894)
Women's rights activist, editor, writer

AMELIA JENKS BLOOMER WAS THE OWNER, editor, and distributor of the first important women's rights newspaper in America. She omitted the word "obey" from her marriage vows when Dexter Chamberlain Bloomer became her husband in 1840. But she was not—originally—an avowed feminist. Even though she attended the 1848 women's rights convention in her hometown of Seneca Falls, New York, at the time she was more interested in temperance. She dedicated her newspaper, *The Lily*, entirely to the temperance cause.

Then, in 1850, the male politicians of Tennessee said that women could not own property because they had no souls. Amelia Bloomer fired off her first editorial on the subject of women's rights. And, from that point on, she devoted as much space in *The Lily* to women's rights issues as to temperance. She commissioned articles from Elizabeth Cady Stanton, Susan B. Anthony, and many other leading women's rights reformers.

Although she stopped publishing *The Lily* when she moved to Iowa in 1855, Bloomer actively campaigned for women's rights for the next four decades. She is usually remembered for the Turkish-style pants that bear her name, even though she didn't invent them. Many 19th-century female reformers, including Stanton and Anthony, enjoyed wearing the comfortable "bloomers" for a time. They stopped when public outcry against the outfit threatened to distract people from other women's rights issues that they found more important.

Susan Elizabeth Blow (1843–1916)
Educator

SUSAN BLOW, THE DAUGHTER OF A ST. LOUIS businessman, encountered the ideas of the kindergarten innovator Friedrich Froebel while traveling in Germany in 1870. Many of Froebel's educational philosophies arose from his religious convictions, which appealed to the profoundly spiritual Blow. She trained in New York City with the Froebel disciple Maria Kraus-Boelte. Then, in 1873, she established the nation's first public kindergarten in St. Louis. By 1880 every public school in the city included a kindergarten.

Froebel's method emphasized self-expression through play and encouraged hands-on activities, such as weaving and modeling with clay. He had also devised songs and games, which Blow translated. In the late 1880s, liberal kindergarten teachers began to adapt and update the songs and games—reforms that Blow vehemently opposed. After 1895 Blow lived mostly in New York. She belonged to the International Kindergarten Union and lectured at Columbia University's Teachers College. Her many books include a translation of Froebel's *Mother Play* (1895) and *Kindergarten Education* (1900).

Barbara Leigh Smith Bodichon (1827–1891)
Educator, women's rights activist, artist

BARBARA LEIGH SMITH CAME FROM A PROGRESSIVE British family. Her father was a believer in equal education for the sexes, and, when Barbara turned 21, he gave her a substantial yearly allowance. She would never be forced to marry to support herself. The next year, she went to London to study art at Bedford College for women.

In London, Barbara entered a social and political whirl. Not even marriage to the French doctor Eugene Bodichon in 1856 limited her activities. As a painter, she knew the important artists and writers of the day. As a reformer, she dedicated herself to many causes.

In 1852 Barbara cofounded the successful Portman Hall School, welcoming a wide range of students, rich and poor, boys and girls. In 1858 she helped establish the feminist *Englishwoman's Journal*. When women came to the journal offices looking for work, Bodichon and her coworkers hired them to operate the printshop that produced the paper. They also formed The Society for Promoting the Employment of Women.

While campaigning for suffrage, Bodichon became friends with Emily Davies, with whom she founded Girton College in 1869. From then on, she worked to promote the school, even after a stroke in 1877 forced her to slow down. At her death, she left Girton a large sum of money, much of which came from the sale of her art.

Maud Ballington Booth (1865–1948)
Social reformer, prison reformer

GROWING UP IN LONDON, MAUD BOOTH WAS upset by the misery she saw in the city's slums. She attended a Salvation Army meeting when she was 16 and was deeply impressed. The Army, established by General William Booth, worked for the needy while spreading Christianity. It was exactly the outlet Maud had been hoping to find. Plenty of churchgoing Christians disapproved of the fiery way General Booth preached in the streets, though. Maud's father, who was a clergyman, didn't speak to her for years after she joined in 1883. Maud married General Booth's son, Ballington Booth, and in 1887 the couple set out to reorganize the American branch of the Salvation Army. In New York City, Maud established many welfare programs. She arranged for workers to live in the slums with the people who needed them most. As a result of the Booths' efforts, the Salvation Army's reputation among Christians improved drastically. Then in 1896, General Booth decided to send them to a different country. Unwilling to abandon their work in America, the Booths resigned. Ballington's sister, Evangeline Cory Booth, took over their position in 1904.

Maud and Ballington formed their own charitable organization, the Volunteers of America. Maud took up prison reform, founding both the Volunteer Prison League and Hope Hall, a halfway house for former prisoners, in 1896. She also participated in the war relief effort during World War I.

Djamila Boupacha (1942–)
Nationalist

DJAMILA BOUPACHA BECAME A HEROINE IN Algeria for her role in the nationalist movement to win her country's independence from France. Born into a middle-class family, Boupacha had received a French education, like many other young Algerians who joined the revolutionary movement and used guerrilla tactics. Accused of throwing a bomb into a café near the University of Algiers, she was arrested in 1961. She was freed the following year when Charles de Gaulle, the president of France, granted Algeria its independence.

After her release, Boupacha brought a lawsuit to protest her treatment. She had endured terrible torture while in prison. This fact received wide public attention when her lawyer, Gisele Halimi, and the French feminist and philosopher, Simone de Beauvoir, wrote a book about her case. Beauvoir also worked with other prominent French intellectuals to organize a Djamila Boupacha Committee. Boupacha has since dedicated herself to expanding women's rights in Algeria.

Myra Colby Bradwell (1831–1894)
Lawyer, publisher, women's rights activist

ALTHOUGH OFFICIALLY THE SECOND FEMALE LAWYER in America, Myra Colby Bradwell was a first-rate pioneer in the field. She laid the groundwork that generations of professional women followed.

Bradwell was born in Vermont, but her family moved several times and eventually settled in Illinois. She started her career as a teacher, then turned her attention to law, one of her longtime interests. She had the support of her husband, James, a successful lawyer himself. In 1868 she launched a journal called the *Chicago Legal News*, for which she served as business manager and editor.

In 1869 Bradwell passed the qualifying exam and applied for admission to the Illinois bar, but the state and—upon appeal—the United States Supreme Court dismissed her application because she was female. Undeterred, Bradwell went on with the *Legal News*. She also worked with her husband to reform marriage laws and end sex discrimination in the workplace. They campaigned for suffrage, temperance, and prison reform. She built such an impressive reputation that, in 1890, the state took the unusual step of seeking her out to admit her to the bar.

The Bradwells lost nearly everything in Chicago's Great Fire of 1871. But their 13-year-old daughter, Bessie, saved the subscription list for the *Legal News*, so it went out as scheduled in spite of the disaster. Bessie later became a lawyer and took over her mother's position at the paper.

Lily Braun (1865–1916)
Early radical feminist, writer

LILY BRAUN WAS A RADICAL AMONG RADICALS, often separated from contemporary male-dominated socialist groups because of her feminist emphasis. She was notorious for her free-wheeling ways, as well as for her political ideals.

Born to a wealthy, Prussian family, Braun was raised to marry an aristocrat. While in her 20s, though, she became involved in several radical groups and joined the Social Democratic party. Like many German feminists of the time, Braun saw motherhood as the supreme human endeavor. She also argued that the positive relationship between mother and child was the cure to the negative master-slave dynamic fostered by capitalism. She dreamed of a society in which all human beings were honored equally.

The book *The Women's Question, Its Historical Development and Its Economic Aspect* (1901) remains her most influential work. She also founded a feminist newspaper, *The Women's Movement*, with Minna Cauer and a weekly, *The New Society*, with her second husband, Heinrich Braun. Her autobiography, *Memoir of a Socialist*, was published in 1908.

Sophonisba Preston Breckinridge (1866–1948)
Social worker, educator, social reformer

SOPHONISBA BRECKINRIDGE WAS BORN IN Lexington, Kentucky, to a prominent political family. Her father was a United States congressman, and her grandfather was Attorney General during the presidency of Thomas Jefferson. And Breckinridge followed their example of public service. In 1895 she became the first practicing woman lawyer in Kentucky but soon decided to pursue further studies. At the University of Chicago in 1901, she earned the first Ph.D. in political science ever given to a woman. She began teaching, and she participated in the reform activities of Jane Addams's Hull House, where she lived from 1907 to 1920.

Breckinridge and Edith Abbott, another Hull House resident, collaborated to study living conditions in Chicago's slums and wrote several books. They also worked together at the newly established Chicago School of Civics and Philanthropy. In the 1920s, they led the transformation of the school into the Graduate School of Social Service Administration, part of the University of Chicago. It remains a leading graduate program for social workers.

As with so many energetic and caring women of her time, Breckinridge was involved in many reform movements, including the fight for child labor laws, women's rights, immigrants' rights, and pacifism. She was a member of the National Association for the Advancement of Colored People and campaigned for the Progressive party in 1912. Breckinridge worked as a teacher and writer until her death.

Margaret Brent (1600?–1671?)
Colonial landowner, lawyer

AS ROMAN CATHOLICS IN PREDOMINANTLY Protestant England, Margaret Brent's family had suffered persecution. So they decided to go to the New World where they could worship freely.

Before leaving, Brent wrote to Lord Baltimore, proprietor of the Maryland colony, asking for a land grant. She received over 70 acres (28 ha) to share with her sister Mary, and in 1638, the sisters and two brothers set sail. Brent began to prosper immediately. A natural businesswoman, she acquired more land in Maryland and Virginia. She acted as an attorney for herself and her family. Step by step, her power grew.

In 1644 a group of Protestants revolted against the colony's Catholic leadership. The governor, Leonard Calvert, retreated to Virginia to gather troops, while Brent assembled an army in Maryland, and in the spring of 1647, they defeated the rebels. Soon afterward Calvert died, giving Brent control of his estate—and leaving her with a problem. The soldiers who had fought to save the colony had never been paid. They were about to start a rebellion of their own. Brent sold some of Calvert's land to settle the debts, which almost got her in trouble with Lord Baltimore back in England. However, the grateful leaders of the colony recognized what she had done and defended her.

At an assembly meeting in 1648, Brent made a formal request. She was the most powerful person in Maryland: a landowner and Lord Baltimore's lawyer, she pointed out. She was entitled to two votes in the assembly. But it was unthinkable that a woman should vote; her request was denied. Brent moved to Virginia, where she continued her successful business ventures.

examination. Although meant to improve the health of military men, the acts did so by ignoring the constitutional rights of poor women. Besides, they effectively approved of men visiting prostitutes while treating the women as criminals. It was an unpopular cause, but Butler courageously campaigned, even when threatened by angry crowds. The acts were repealed in 1886, and the movement is usually referred to as "Josephine Butler's campaign." Butler also fought against the white slave trade of the 1880s. She wrote widely, including the book *Personal Reminiscences of a Great Crusade* (1896).

Josephine Grey Butler (1828–1906)
Social reformer, women's rights leader

JOSEPHINE BUTLER ADDRESSED THE PROBLEM OF prostitution from the heart. She recognized that poor women who turned to this degrading way of life were not evil. Instead, they needed better educational and employment opportunities. Butler turned to reform work as a way to ease her anguish over her five-year-old daughter's death from an accidental fall. In 1866 she opened the House of Rest, a shelter for destitute women. From 1868 to 1873, she led the North of England Council for Promoting the Higher Education of Women.

Butler became famous for her opposition to the Contagious Diseases Acts of 1864, 1866, and 1869. Under these laws, any woman suspected of prostitution was subjected to arrest and physical

Frances Xavier Cabrini (1850–1917)
Religious leader, humanitarian

BORN IN ITALY, MARIA FRANCESCA CABRINI WAS still just a girl when she decided to devote her life to the Catholic religion. She became a teacher at the age of 18. By the time she was 24, as a result of her work at an orphanage in Codogno, Italy, she was already known as "Mother Cabrini."

Cabrini became a nun in 1877, taking the name Frances Xavier. Then, instead of joining an established convent, she founded her own religious order, the Missionary Sisters of the Sacred Heart of Jesus, in 1880. In 1889, having already established a number of convents in Italy, Cabrini considered traveling to China. But Pope Leo XIII convinced her to look to the United States. There, more and more impoverished Italian immigrants needed her help. Mother

Cabrini and the six nuns she took with her to New York wasted no time getting started. Within a month, they opened an orphanage. After that, Cabrini established orphanages, schools, convents, and hospitals in the United States, Latin America, and Europe.

By the time she died in 1917, over 1,500 women had taken vows to become Missionary Sisters, and they operated more than 65 houses of charity. By providing services within Italian communities and in the native language, Cabrini's institutions made it possible for immigrants to receive much needed help. Naturalized as a United States citizen in 1909, Mother Cabrini was the first American to be named a saint, in 1946.

Donaldina Mackenzie Cameron (1869–1968)
Mission superintendent

WHEN DONALDINA CAMERON BEGAN MISSIONARY work, secret Chinese societies called "tongs" were at the height of their power. The tongs had established a slave trade in young girls, tricking them into leaving China with tales of a better life in America, then selling them as wives or prostitutes to Chinese men living in San Francisco. Cameron was determined to bring this practice to an end.

Cameron was born in New Zealand to Scottish parents. Her father, a sheep rancher, brought his family to northern California in 1871. She considered

becoming a teacher but couldn't afford college. In 1895 she got a job at a home run by the Woman's Occidental Board of Foreign Missions and, by 1900, she was superintendent.

Known to the tongs as "Fahn Quai" ("White Devil") and to those she rescued as "Lo Mo" ("Mother"), Cameron had a reputation for fearlessness. She ignored death threats, wore disguises to perform rescues, and led police to brothel doors so they could smash them down. Less glamorous but equally important were her court battles for custody of many girls, whom she raised as foster daughters. As slavery became less of a problem, Cameron expanded the community programs at the mission.

Cameron stayed at the mission until she reached the age of 65, when she was required to retire. In 1942 the mission to which she had dedicated so many years was named Donaldina Cameron House in her honor.

Rosario Castellanos (1925–1974)
Reformer, writer, teacher, diplomat

BORN IN MEXICO CITY, ROSARIO CASTELLANOS spent her girlhood in the small town of Comitán in Chiapas. Her family was forced to move in 1941, when their property became part of a campaign to return land to native groups, but Castellanos always considered the area her home.

In the 1950s Castellanos returned to Chiapas to work in the Indian community and embraced

the native culture she had known as a child. While there, she worked to promote literacy, performed with a traveling theater group that addressed social issues, and wrote pamphlets that explained Indians' legal rights. She also finished writing her first novel, *Balún-Canán* (1957, published in English as *The Nine Guardians*), a look at Tzotzil Indian culture through the eyes of a little girl.

Castellanos expressed her strong feminist and social consciousness in all of her literary works. Many of her stories publicized the plight of native peoples. In recognition of her public service, she was named Mexican Ambassador to Israel in 1971 and served until her untimely death three years later.

Carrie Chapman Catt (1859–1947)
Suffragist, pacifist

IN 1900 CARRIE CHAPMAN CATT WAS PICKED BY Susan B. Anthony to lead the National American Woman Suffrage Association. Catt was a respected speaker and an organizational wizard, not to mention a visionary reformer. Her husband had so much faith in her that he signed a document before they married, allowing her to dedicate a third of every year to reform work. Catt served as president of NAWSA for four years, then stepped down. She wanted to concentrate on the fight for suffrage at an international level and begin to work for world peace.

But without Catt, NAWSA fell prey to the same disputes about political strategy that had always plagued the suffrage movement. People began to break away from the group. Worried that the cause was in danger, in 1915, NAWSA members begged Catt to return as their president. She agreed and began a campaign targeted at both state and federal governments. She taught suffragists how to lobby congressmen. During World War I, she made sure that NAWSA members joined the war effort. This showed them to be patriotic, respectable citizens.

Even after women cast their first legal votes in 1920, Catt continued to lead. She transformed the NAWSA into the League of Women Voters to educate women about political issues in preparation for casting their ballots. And she returned to pacifist work. In addition to the Woman's Peace party she helped found in 1915, she established the Committee on the Cause and Cure of War in 1925, and the Protest Committee of Non-Jewish Women Against the Persecution of the Jews in 1933.

Chai Ling (1966–)
Leader in Chinese democracy movement

IN 1989 A MOVEMENT AROSE AMONG STUDENTS IN Beijing, China, to demand democratic reforms from the Communist government. Each day more protesters joined the cause, staging hunger strikes and sit-ins in Tiananmen Square. One of these protesters was Chai Ling, who was elected student commander of the movement in April.

Then on June 3rd, the government sent tanks to the square. Chai encouraged the students to stand their ground and remain peaceful. Suddenly, the lights went out and bullets flew. It is still not known how many people—perhaps thousands—were killed during the 24 hours that followed. Afterward, realizing they were in great danger, Chai and her husband, activist Feng Congde, vanished.

Supportive strangers helped to conceal them for ten months, until they finally escaped China. Then they made their way to America. Chai has since finished her education at Princeton University, and she continues to work for democracy in her homeland. It is a difficult and often lonely task. She is still on China's "most wanted" list and may never see her family again. She and her husband have divorced.

Chai Ling is not without critics. Some say that she should not have encouraged students to face the troops, that she should have stayed in the country, that she enjoys being a celebrity. But her many supporters don't hesitate to applaud the brave effort she made against overwhelming odds.

Ch'iu Chin (1875?–1907)
Revolutionary, feminist

CH'IU CHIN IS A HEROINE OF THE TURN-OF-THE-century revolutionary movement in China, where she is still revered for her bravery, military skill, and intense personality. She not only wrote poetry but boxed, fenced, rode horses, and wore men's clothing.

Raised in a middle-class family, Ch'iu Chin entered into a traditional arranged marriage, but her attitude was progressive. She spoke against the custom of binding girls' feet to stop them from growing. Moving to Peking in 1900, she was outraged that the Manchu rulers under Empress Tz'u Hsi lived in luxury while the people were terribly poor. In 1903 she went to Tokyo, Japan, and joined a revolutionary group headed by Sun Yat-sen.

Returning to China in 1906, she started a feminist newspaper and a branch of the revolutionary Restoration Society. In 1907, as principal of the Ta-t'ung School of Physical Culture in Shao-hsing, she turned her students into soldiers, drilling them

> "The perfume of freedom burns my mind
> With grief for my country.
> When will we ever be cleansed?
> Comrades, I say to you,
> Spare no effort, struggle unceasingly,
> That at last peace may come to our people.
> And jeweled dresses and deformed feet
> Will be abandoned.
> And one day, all under heaven
> Will see beautiful free women,
> Blooming like fields of flowers,
> And bearing brilliant and noble human beings."
>
> CH'IU CHIN, from a poem
> to the tune "The River Is Red,"
> translated by Kenneth Rexroth

for her planned uprising. At the last minute, though, word of the impending rebellion reached the government, and Ch'iu Chin was captured and executed. The Manchu dynasty she had opposed was toppled just four years later.

Septima Poinsette Clark (1898–1987)
Educator, civil rights activist

IN 1956 SEPTIMA POINSETTE CLARK, A BLACK teacher with 40 years of hard-won experience, was fired by the Charleston Board of Education. Her commitment to educating blacks about their political rights made many southern whites nervous. A South Carolina law had recently been passed forbidding government workers to join the NAACP, and Clark had been brave enough to state her membership publicly. So she paid with her job.

Clark moved to Tennessee to teach at the Highlander Folk School, which offered literacy classes for adults. The organizers of the school agreed with her that education was the path to liberation, and they made her feel at home. They also supported her when she opened her first "Citizenship School" on St. John's Island, South Carolina. She went on to open several others as well.

In 1961 Martin Luther King, Jr. persuaded Clark to train civil rights workers at the schools, and she began working under the sponsorship of the Southern Christian Leadership Conference. She helped coordinate the Voter Education Project from 1962 to 1965. The program taught black people how to handle the deliberately misleading questions that were often asked at qualifying tests for voter registration. By the time Clark retired in 1970, she could rest secure in the knowledge that she had brought the seeds of change to future generations of African Americans.

Frances Power Cobbe (1822–1904)
Women's rights activist, animal rights activist

FRANCES POWER COBBE SUBSCRIBED TO THE common Victorian belief that women were by nature morally superior to men. She used this socially acceptable attitude to support her feminist

ideals, arguing that the moral viewpoint should have stronger representation in the public arena.

Born and educated in Ireland, Cobbe lived at home until her father's death in 1857 allowed her to travel and indulge her broad interests. She particularly loved Italy, and was the Italian correspondent for the British newspaper *The Echo* from 1868 to 1875.

A philanthropist with many connections among wealthy families, Cobbe worked with poor children at Mary Carpenter's Red Lodge Reformatory school in Bristol, England. She took up feminist issues during the 1860s, writing and lecturing in favor of women's suffrage, university education for women, and greater legal rights for married women. In the last half of her life, she turned her attention to animal protection, calling for an end to the suffering caused by dissecting live animals for scientific experiments. She cofounded the two main English antivivisection organizations, wrote books about animal protection, and edited the journal *Zoophilist*. Her books include *The Duties of Women* (1881) and *The Life of Frances Power Cobbe by Herself* (1894).

Johnnetta Betsch Cole (1936–)
Educator, anthropologist

A S A YOUNG GIRL IN JACKSONVILLE, FLORIDA, Johnnetta Cole was surrounded by supportive family. Her grandfather had been a prominent citizen in town, and her professional parents sent all three of their children to college. On the other hand, as an African American in the South of the 1940s, there was plenty that Cole couldn't do. The swimming pool across the street from her childhood home would have been a great hangout on hot summer days—except that it was whites-only.

An exceptional and motivated student, Cole entered Fisk University at age 15, then joined her sister at Oberlin College in Ohio the following year. She received a Ph.D. in anthropology from Northwestern University in 1969 and went on to teach at the university level. Through her teaching and anthropological fieldwork, focusing on culture and women's roles, she has played an important role in establishing both African American studies and women's studies as academic fields.

In 1987 she was named the first black female president of Spelman College for women, a position she held for ten years. Cole, who has five sons, referred to her students at Spelman as her "daughters" and to herself as the "sister president." She currently teaches anthropology at Emory University in Atlanta, Georgia, and serves on the boards of numerous foundations, educational institutions, and corporations.

Jill Kathryn Ker Conway (1934–)
Writer, historian, educator

J ILL KER CONWAY BEGAN LIFE AT HER PARENTS' sheep station in New South Wales, Australia. After graduating from the University of Sydney in 1958, she earned her Ph.D. from Harvard in 1969. Her pioneering doctoral dissertation traced the history of Jane Addams and other top female reformers of America's Progressive Era.

By 1972 Conway was an associate professor at the University of Toronto in Canada, and she went on to become vice-president. During the student uprisings of the mid-1970s, she demonstrated her competence as an administrator, and that led to her appointment as the first woman president of Smith College in 1975. During her ten years at Smith, Conway increased the college's endowment from $82 million to $220 million. She opened scholarships to working women and women on welfare. Smith also became the first women's college to join the National Collegiate Athletic Association while she was at the helm. In addition to her rigorous administrative schedule, Conway regularly taught a course on contemporary American feminist thought.

Today Conway is a visiting scholar at the Massachusetts Institute of Technology. Her books include *The Road from Coorain* (1989) and *When Memory Speaks: Reflections on Autobiography* (1998).

Mairead Corrigan-Maguire (1944–)
Social worker, pacifist

SOMETIMES A TERRIBLE EVENT STIRS PEOPLE TO ACT as leaders. On August 10, 1976, a woman was out walking with her four children in Belfast, Northern Ireland. Suddenly a car, racing out of control, crashed onto the sidewalk. Its driver, a 19-year-old member of the Irish Republican Army, had just been shot by British soldiers. Three of the children on the sidewalk were killed. Their mother was Mairead Corrigan-Maguire's sister.

Mairead Corrigan-Maguire (right) with Betty Williams

Corrigan-Maguire was already a welfare worker, concerned with helping Catholic youth in Belfast. After the death of her niece and two nephews, she became a public figure. Within a week, she joined a witness to the accident, Betty Williams, in calling for a peaceful solution to the violence between Catholics and Protestants. At their urging, 10,000 women of both religions marched to visit the children's graves.

Corrigan-Maguire and Williams helped to form the Community of Peace People. They reasoned that if Protestants and Catholics went to the same schools and lived in the same neighborhoods, they would soon come to respect each other. Every Saturday for months, thousands of Peace People risked their lives marching down roads controlled by armed gunmen. Their success was swift. Within a year, violence decreased 70 percent.

Corrigan-Maguire and Williams received the 1976 Nobel Peace Prize for their outstanding efforts. Unfortunately, the tragic car accident indirectly caused yet another death in January 1980, when Corrigan-Maguire's still-grieving sister committed suicide. Corrigan-Maguire continues to work with the Peace People to inspire young people everywhere to demand a nonviolent world.

Prudence Crandall (1803–1890)
Educator, abolitionist

IN 1831 PRUDENCE CRANDALL, A QUAKER TEACHER, opened a girls' academy in Canterbury, Connecticut, and it quickly earned an excellent reputation. Then her troubles began. Crandall admitted the daughter of a neighboring farmer, who was black. Horrified, the white families quickly withdrew their daughters from class. Crandall, who had the support of prominent abolitionists such as William Lloyd Garrison, responded by opening a school exclusively for black girls, and the entire town turned against her. The doctor even refused to visit her house if someone got sick.

The strong-willed Crandall persisted, so the townspeople enacted a law that required anyone who wanted to educate black children to apply for special permission from the local authorities. Crandall spent a few months in jail as a result. Returning to the academy, she encountered obstacle after obstacle. Someone contaminated her drinking water with manure; somebody else tried to set her house on fire; and a mob stormed the building.

At last, in 1834, Crandall closed the school. The continual persecution had made it impossible for her to concentrate on teaching. In 1842 she and her husband moved away and settled in Illinois. Decades later, the Connecticut legislature voted to give the 83-year-old Crandall a small pension in an effort to make up for her ordeal.

Nancy Cunard (1896–1965)
Publisher, civil rights campaigner, writer

NANCY CUNARD, A BRITISH HEIRESS FROM A family that owned a line of steamships, founded the Hours Press in Paris in 1928. Within a year, she and the jazz pianist Henry Crowder had conceived an ambitious project, an anthology of writings about black culture, art, and politics. It took years to complete, especially amid the scandal of her romantic relationship with Crowder, who was black. Many of the most influential writers of the day contributed, including Zora Neale Hurston, Ezra Pound, W. E. B. Du Bois, and Langston Hughes. The book *Negro* appeared in 1934, and as it turned out,

documented much of the discrimination she and Crowder had encountered while compiling it.

Cunard was one of the most outspoken European defenders of the "Scottsboro Boys," nine black men falsely accused of raping two white women in Alabama in 1931. She wrote articles and planned fund-raising events, such as an interracial dance, to support their cause. Crowder moved to America in the mid-1930s, but Cunard stayed in Europe, writing, editing, and promoting the causes she believed in.

Mary Daly (1928–)
Radical feminist writer, philosopher, theologian

MARY DALY'S OUTLOOK ON MALE-DOMINATED society is unique. In her book, *Gyn/Ecology* (1978), she argues that language itself is oppressive to women and creates over 200 new words in an effort to break out of that oppression.

Daly, born an Irish-Catholic, has played a leading role in bringing women's spiritual health into public debate. Though denied entry to the University of Notre Dame in the early 1950s because she was a woman, Daly went on to earn three doctorates in theology and philosophy, two from the University of Fribourg in Switzerland.

Although Daly is academically well respected, her outspoken and unconventional views have attracted criticism. She has repeatedly been denied full professorship at Boston College, where she has taught for over 30 years. In 1968 she was fired from the school after she published *The Church and the Second Sex.* The book's in-depth critique of women's place within the Catholic religion caused an uproar, but she also won many people over with her argument. Student outrage at her dismissal influenced the school to rehire her in 1969—with tenure and a promotion.

Daly's radical examination of religion and modern society forms the center of all her books. Her published works include *Beyond God the Father* (revised 1985) and, most recently, *Pure Lust: Elemental Feminist Philosophy* (1998).

Emily Davies (1830–1921)
Educator, feminist

EMILY DAVIES WAS CONVINCED THAT WOMEN'S intelligence was the same as men's, and that they deserved the same educational opportunities. She disagreed with many women's rights activists of her day, who believed that women might be equally intelligent, but in a different— feminine—way.

Davies first put her ideas to work after meeting Barbara Bodichon and the doctor Elizabeth Garrett Anderson during a visit to London in 1859. Inspired, she returned to her home in northern England and worked to promote women's employment. By 1861 she had moved to London, where she edited a feminist paper, worked with John Stuart Mill on the first women's suffrage petition, founded the London Schoolmistresses' Association, and served on the London School Board.

In 1869 Davies and Bodichon joined together to found a college where women could study classics and math, just as men did. The students proved their muster at exam time, too. And many of them went on to teach at the university level. Within four years, the institution had been renamed Girton College and made a part of Cambridge University. Davies dedicated herself to Girton for over four decades. Her collection of essays, *Thoughts on Some Questions Relating to Women, 1860–1908* (1910) provides an overview of the issues she addressed in her long career.

Angela Yvonne Davis (1944–)
Radical activist, educator, philosopher

GROWING UP IN ALABAMA DURING SEGREGATION, Angela Davis experienced prejudice from the beginning. Racially motivated bombings against blacks were not uncommon in her neighborhood. Instead of giving up, though, Davis's parents kept active in local politics. They encouraged their daughter to follow their example and to seek a good education.

At graduate school in San Diego, Davis worked for civil rights, women's rights, and prison reform. She opposed the Vietnam War. In 1968 she joined the Communist party, and when she was hired to teach philosophy at the University of California, Los Angeles, Governor Ronald Reagan campaigned to have her fired. He was convinced that her politics were dangerous.

Davis soon had a bigger problem than the fight for her job. Working for black prisoners' rights, she had become associated with a group called the Soledad Brothers. In 1970 the Soledad Brothers were brought to court for trial and tried to escape. A terrible shootout followed, killing four people. Davis, accused of helping to plan the escape, was arrested. She spent 16 months in jail before she was acquitted in 1972.

After her release, Davis resumed her activities with as much energy as ever. She wrote several books, including *Women, Culture and Politics* (1989). In 1980 and 1984, she ran for vice-president of the United States on the Communist ticket. Today she teaches at the University of California at Santa Cruz.

Dorothy Day (1897–1980)
Social activist, journalist

IN 1972 DOROTHY DAY WAS AWARDED A MEDAL from the University of Notre Dame for "comforting the afflicted and afflicting the comforted virtually all her life." It was an accurate assessment. Day simply refused to believe that social problems many people took for granted could not be resolved, and she always backed up her ideas with action.

A member of the Socialist party and the Industrial Workers of the World from the age of 19, Day wrote for New York newspapers such as the *Call* and the

Liberator. She was arrested in 1917 with Alice Paul for protesting America's entry into World War I. In 1927, after she gave birth to her daughter, she converted to Catholicism. Five years later she began working with the French Catholic reformer Peter Maurin. Among Maurin's ideas was the "house of hospitality," where people who were unemployed or needy would live together, along with reformers, in a supportive community. Day and Maurin also started a penny paper together. *The Catholic Worker*, which they distributed on street corners, inspired reforms and openings of hospitality houses across the country.

Day held firm to her pacifist beliefs through World War II, the Cold War, and the Korean and Vietnamese wars. Living in voluntary poverty, she traveled constantly, attending demonstrations and protests. She was arrested for the last time at the age of 75, for attending a strike by César Chávez's United Farm Workers.

Princess Diana of Wales (1961–1997)
Humanitarian

PRINCESS DIANA—THE MOST PHOTOGRAPHED woman in the world—used the camera's flash to illuminate the needs of those who were in the pictures with her. At a time when many were afraid even to touch people who had AIDS, she visited the AIDS ward of a hospital and made a point of holding the patients' hands. Footage taken just weeks before her death showed the Princess talking to Bosnian war victims and contributed to the progress of the 1997 treaty to ban land mines.

When Lady Diana Frances Spencer married Prince Charles on July 29, 1981, nearly a billion people watched the televised wedding, enthralled by the fairy-tale life of the aristocratic 20 year old. Diana's warm personality put a human face on the regal duties she performed. Many admired her uninhibited displays of affection for her sons, William and Harry, as well as her determination to guard them from the oppressive attention of the media.

When it was learned that her personal life was full of torment that included loneliness, depression, suicidal thoughts, and an eating disorder known as bulimia, the public became, if anything, more adoring. The royal couple divorced in 1996, and Diana

renounced all claim to becoming Queen of England. She had just begun to devote herself to humanitarian causes when her life was tragically cut short by a car accident in Paris, France, on August 31, 1997.

Dorothea Lynde Dix (1802–1887)
Social reformer, advocate for the mentally ill

THE IDEA THAT MENTAL ILLNESS IS A DISEASE IS familiar today, but this wasn't true in the 19th century. Then, "lunatics" were considered unmanageable, even inhuman. They were often kept in chains and cages. Dorothea Dix made it her life's work to give mentally ill people better treatment.

Dix took on adult responsibilities at an early age. Because her mother was sickly, she cared for her younger siblings until she was 12. When she was only 14, she opened a girls' school in Worcester, Massachusetts. Dix taught for many years and also wrote children's books, but she had to stop teaching full-time in 1836 because of poor health. One Sunday in 1841, Dix went to the jail in East Cambridge, Massachusetts, to teach a Bible class. There, she found mentally ill women confined with criminals in filthy conditions—and the "madwomen" hadn't even broken the law. Dix went to the local court and convinced officials to provide heat and clean the cells.

Then she visited every jail and poorhouse in Massachusetts, carefully recording her observations. She presented the long list of her shocking findings to the state legislature. As a result, the state opened institutions where the mentally ill could live. Dix persuaded many states to open mental hospitals and even took her campaign abroad. She only interrupted her work during the Civil War, when she served as superintendent of Army nurses. Thanks to Dix's leadership, people began to think more about the ways they could help the mentally ill.

Anna Murray Douglass (1813?–1882)
Abolitionist

ANNA MURRAY DOUGLASS IS OFTEN OVERLOOKED in history books. However, she played a significant role in freeing slaves by means of the Underground Railroad. And if it weren't for her ingenuity, her famous husband, Frederick Douglass, might never have made it to the North.

A free black, Anna Murray met the slave Frederick Bailey at a church social in Baltimore. She used all her savings—nine years' worth—and helped to disguise him as a sailor to escape to New York in 1838. They changed their name to Douglass after marriage.

Douglass was often left alone while Frederick lectured for the abolitionists. She ran the household, raised their children, arranged all their finances, and worked for abolition in Massachusetts and New York. Her home was a stop for escaped slaves on their way to freedom along the Underground Railroad.

The most detailed account of her life was written by the Douglasses' oldest child, Rosetta, who notes that her mother, who was illiterate for her entire life, "could not be known all at once, she had to be studied."

Abigail Scott Duniway (1834–1915)
Suffragist, newspaper publisher

AS A CHILD, THEN AS A WIFE AND MOTHER OF SIX, Abigail Duniway knew how hard a woman's life could be. At age 18, she made the difficult journey with her family from Illinois to Oregon. In 1862 Duniway's husband lost their farm and then suffered a severe accident, so she became their sole support. She opened a boarding school, then a shop. All the while, she thought about how she could improve the conditions of women's lives.

In 1871 Duniway decided to take action. Moving her family to Portland, she founded the Oregon State Woman Suffrage Association and started the *New Northwest*, a newspaper dedicated to women's rights and suffrage.

Though Duniway was the leading supporter of women's rights in Oregon, Idaho, and Washington, she often disagreed with the activities of the National Woman Suffrage Association. She didn't like the way NWSA organizers linked voting rights with other reforms, especially temperance. For Duniway suffrage was the most important issue at hand, and she felt more men would support the cause if it stood alone.

Idaho and Washington both approved women's suffrage before Oregon did. An 1884 referendum failed there, as did other bids in 1900, 1906, 1908, and 1910. Finally in 1912, Duniway joyfully became the first woman in the state to register.

Andrea Dworkin (1946–)
Radical feminist, writer

ANDREA DWORKIN IS AN INTENSELY PRIVATE person, but she consistently makes issues public that many consider too intimate to discuss. She has become best known for her unswerving opposition to pornography. Her stance has inspired both admiration and wrath from feminists.

Dworkin was born in Camden, New Jersey, and attended Bennington College in Vermont. In 1974 she published the first of her many books, *Woman Hating*, in which she examined cultural practices that have oppressed women throughout history. Among other topics, she discussed the Chinese tradition of binding women's feet, witch-hunts, and the passivity of female fairy-tale characters. That same year, Dworkin was invited to attend a National Organization for Women convention and delivered her first major speech, receiving a standing ovation.

Dworkin joined lawyer Catherine MacKinnon in 1983 to work for legislation banning pornography on the grounds that it discriminates against women. They coauthored *Pornography and Civil Rights* in 1988, but many people balked at their call for censorship. The First Amendment's protection of free speech has led to their bill's defeat in the courts, but they still hope to find a solution to the problem. A resident of Brooklyn, Dworkin writes fiction as well as nonfiction.

Crystal Eastman (1881–1928)
Labor lawyer, journalist, social reformer

CRYSTAL EASTMAN CALLED HERSELF A "COMPLETE feminist." She believed that women could be equal to men in every way. She worked tirelessly to live up to that standard, devoting herself not only to feminist issues but to the cause of freedom in general. As she wrote in 1920, "Freedom is a large word."

Tall, athletic Eastman had a master's in sociology from Columbia University and a law degree from New York University. She worked with Lillian Wald at the Henry Street Settlement and Alice Paul of the National Woman's party. Her book *Work Accidents and the Law* (1910) influenced the establishment of workers' compensation laws. After World War I began, she helped found the National Women's Peace party. And with her brother, Max Eastman, she cofounded and wrote for the socialist and pacifist paper, *The Liberator*.

One of Eastman's most enduring contributions is the result of her work with the American Union Against Militarism, founded in 1916 by Wald and others. As executive director of the AUAM, Eastman worked with Roger Baldwin to set up a special unit, the National Civil Liberties Bureau. Its purpose was to defend the rights of Americans who, for reasons of conscience, refused to participate in militaristic activities. The Bureau later became the American Civil Liberties Union, which defends freedom of speech and thought to this day.

Mary Baker Eddy (1821–1910)
Religious leader, publisher

MARY BAKER EDDY SPENT MOST OF HER EARLY life seeking relief from illness. Even as a little girl, she had been frail. Suddenly widowed at age 22, poor and sickly, she was forced to give up her first and only child for adoption. Then in 1862, she went to see Phineas P. Quimby in Maine. Quimby was a "mental healer," who treated his patients by thinking positive thoughts as he placed his hands on their heads. Right away, Eddy felt better than she had in years. Impressed, she began to study to become a healer herself.

In January 1866, Quimby died. Eddy was devastated and—to make matters worse—she slipped on ice and injured her back just a month later. A conventional doctor told her she would never walk again. But, amazingly, Eddy was on her feet a few days later, after reading a passage from the Bible.

Combining Quimby's ideas with her religious experience, Eddy concluded that a prayerful mind could heal the body and began to speak about this in public. By 1875 many followers attended weekly meetings at her house, and she published a book, *Science and Health*. She married Asa Eddy, one of her most devoted disciples, two years later.

By the time Eddy died at the age of 89, her Church of Christ (Scientist) was a formal religion with tens of thousands of faithful members. The newspaper she had founded in 1908, *The Christian Science Monitor*, was read across the country. Both the church and the paper remain active today.

> "Service was as essential a part of my upbringing as eating and sleeping and going to school. The church was a hub of Black children's social existence, and caring Black adults were buffers against the segregated and hostile outside world that told us we weren't important. But our parents said it wasn't so, our teachers said it wasn't so, and our preacher said it wasn't so. The message of my racially segregated childhood was clear: let no man or woman look down on you, and look down on no man or woman."
>
> MARIAN WRIGHT EDELMAN
> *The Measure of Our Success*

Marian Wright Edelman (1939–)
Children's rights advocate, civil rights lawyer

GROWING UP IN BENNETTSVILLE, SOUTH CAROLINA, Marian Edelman's minister father always encouraged her to help others in the community. She went to Spelman College in the late 1950s and spent her junior year in Europe, where she enjoyed the sense of freedom. "I wasn't prepared to go back to a segregated existence," she later said, explaining why she became so active in civil rights sit-ins and protests in Atlanta during her last year of college.

Deciding to become a civil rights lawyer, Edelman earned her degree from Yale in 1963. She then went to Mississippi, where she worked as head of the NAACP Legal Defense and Education Fund and was the first black woman to pass the Mississippi bar. Moving to Washington, D.C., in 1968, she started the Washington Research Project to study poverty issues.

In 1973 Edelman founded the Children's Defense Fund to bring the plight of struggling families and children to national attention. With the federal budget cuts of the 1990s, Edelman's efforts to improve the health, welfare, and legal rights of children have expanded. She led the first Stand for Children rally in 1996, bringing over 250,000 demonstrators together at the Lincoln Memorial. The annual event now occurs on or around June 1st in cities nationwide. Edelman's many articles and books include *The Measure of Our Success: A Letter to My Children and Yours* (1992).

Dame Millicent Garrett Fawcett (1847–1929)
Suffragist

IN 1897 MILLICENT GARRETT FAWCETT BECAME president of the National Union of Women's Suffrage Societies in England, adopting the motto: "Faith, Perseverance, Patience." She would need that patience. She not only had to change the attitudes of men who firmly believed women had no place in politics. She also had to convince many moderate people that not all suffragists used the violent tactics associated with Emmeline and Christabel Pankhurst. And even after Parliament passed a law in 1918 allowing women to vote, it took ten more years before they were given full political equality. By then, Fawcett had been working for suffrage for over half a century.

Fawcett's perseverance and patience may have been family traits. Her older sister, Elizabeth Garrett Anderson, struggled for years to become the first practicing female doctor in England. Their father, Newson Garrett, a political radical, was a source of constant encouragement during that time.

In addition to her suffragist career, Fawcett wrote a popular textbook entitled *Political Economy for Beginners* (1870). She also helped found Newnham College for women at Cambridge in 1871. For her service to Britain during the Boer War in South Africa and World War I, she was given the title of "Dame," the female equivalent of a knight.

Margaret Fell (1614–1702)
Religious writer

MARGARET FELL, OFTEN REFERRED TO AS THE "mother" of Quakerism, adopted the religion after meeting the founder of the Society of Friends, George Fox, in 1652. Although her husband, Thomas Fell, did not convert, their home at Swarthmore Hall in Ulverston, England, became a hub of Quaker activity.

Quakers, or Friends, believed that the way to know God was by private revelation. They rejected formal priests, the ceremony of the church, participation in war, and the payment of taxes to the English church. As a result, they were persecuted by the government.

Fell was one of the organizers of the Kendal Fund, which paid the travel costs and prison expenses of Quakers who had been arrested. In 1663 she journeyed 1,000 miles (1,600 km) across England, talking about the Society of Friends. Over the years, she wrote letters to Oliver Cromwell and subsequent rulers of England, arguing for religious tolerance and the release of those imprisoned for their Quaker beliefs. Fell herself was arrested for holding meetings in her home. She used the jail time to write many pamphlets, including *Women's Speaking Justified* (1666). In 1669, 11 years after the death of her first husband, Fell married George Fox.

Vera Nikolayevna Figner (1852–1942)
Revolutionary

DURING THE 1870S, THOUSANDS OF EDUCATED young Russians left the cities and traveled through the countryside urging the peasants to revolt against Czar Alexander II. Vera Figner quit medical school in Switzerland to be a part of this movement. She became a member of the terrorist Narodnaya Volya, or People's Will party, and participated in the assassination of the czar in 1881. Figner managed to escape arrest for nearly two years, but was captured in February 1883.

Her original death sentence was changed to life imprisonment, and Figner spent 20 years in solitary confinement. During this time, she wrote her memoirs, *When the Clock of Life Stopped*, finally published in 1921. After 1906 she lived in exile in Switzerland until she was able to return home in 1915. There, she dedicated herself to social work and writing. Following the Russian Revolution of 1917, Figner was made chairperson of the Amnesty Committee to assist freed political prisoners. She was one of the heroines of the Soviet Union.

Elizabeth Gurley Flynn (1890–1964)
Labor organizer, radical

ONE SUMMER AFTERNOON IN 1906, ELIZABETH Gurley Flynn—then just 16 years old—delivered a speech so powerful that it stopped traffic in New York's Broadway theater district. Her political activism was a legacy from her radical parents: Her Irish-born mother, especially, came from a family that had fought for generations against British control of their country. As a socialist, Flynn believed that the oppressed—women and workers—would never achieve full equality in a capitalist society.

As a member of the Industrial Workers of the World, Flynn played a major role in the 1912 textile strike in Lawrence, Massachusetts, helping Margaret Sanger look after the safety of the strikers' children and attracting media attention to the successful but violent struggle. During World War I, she fought for the civil rights of political prisoners. In 1920 she was present at the founding of the American Civil Liberties Union, a group dedicated to safeguarding free speech. She joined the American Communist party in 1936, and often contributed articles about women's rights to their newspaper, *The Daily Worker*.

Her political activities led to her own imprisonment in the mid-1950s for "conspiring" to overthrow the government. But she remained true to her beliefs. She became the first female head of the American Communist party in 1961.

Betty Naomi Friedan (1921–)
Feminist, journalist

Well-educated, married, and financially comfortable, young Betty Friedan seemed to have it all. Instead, she was miserable. She lost her job as a reporter when she had her second child, and her work as a freelance writer was unsatisfying. Friedan wondered if her other well-off friends felt the same way. So in 1957, she sent questionnaires to 200 homemakers and learned she was not alone.

The book she wrote after researching the issue further—*The Feminine Mystique* (1963)—received extravagant praise, and criticism. In it, Friedan challenged the middle-class idea that a woman's happiness depended on marriage and motherhood. It was a trick, she said: that wasn't always enough. She encouraged women to seek education and work outside the home.

In 1966 Friedan cofounded the National Organization for Women (NOW) to campaign for women's complete equality with men. Even among other feminists, though, she aroused controversy.

Many disagreed with Friedan's focus on middle-class, and therefore primarily white, issues. The dispute led to her resignation in 1970, after four years as NOW's first president.

Friedan continued to observe American culture. In 1981 she wrote *The Second Stage*, pointing out that young feminist "superwomen," who juggled motherhood and a profession, had also been tricked out of happiness, but in a different way from women in earlier eras. At age 72, Friedan published *The Fountain of Age* (1993), in which she discussed the role of the elderly in a culture obsessed with youth.

Elizabeth Fry (1780–1845)
Prison reformer

Elizabeth Fry, a Quaker minister and mother of ten children, first visited London's Newgate Prison in 1813. Hundreds of half-naked women were crowded into the cramped, filthy cells. Many inmates' children lived there, too, and everyone slept on the floor. Appalled, Fry enlisted the help of other wealthy women. They donated money and supplies, and taught prisoners to read, write, and sew. She set up a store stocked with garments made by the inmates, giving them part of the profit when items sold and the rest upon their release. Securing mops, soap, and rags, she instituted a cleaning schedule.

Fry turned her attention to other prisons. Starting in England, then extending her work to other parts of Europe, she inspected facilities and recommended improvements. So successful was her reform work that, even before her death, most prisons in Europe—and some hospitals, mental institutions, and housing projects—had been changed for the better.

Matilda Joslyn Gage (1826–1898)
Women's rights advocate, historian, writer

Matilda Joslyn Gage received an excellent education from her reform-minded father, learning "male" subjects such as math, physiology, and Greek. She married Henry Gage in 1845 and devoted the next several years to raising and educating her four children.

Starting her reform career, Gage made a good impression as the youngest speaker at the 1852 National Woman's Rights Convention in Syracuse. However, she preferred writing to making public appearances. She joined Elizabeth Cady Stanton and Susan B. Anthony's National Woman Suffrage Association at its founding in 1869 and wrote for the suffragist newspaper *The Revolution*. She also helped Stanton and Anthony with their multivolume *History of Woman Suffrage* (1881–1886). As a historian, Gage was concerned that so few female figures were recognized by scholars. Her pioneering book, *Woman as Inventor* (1870), credits women as being innovators in such accomplishments as embroidery, bread-making, and medicine.

Over time, Gage concluded that organized religion was the strongest force keeping women down and that the NWSA was too conservative. So in 1890, she formed the Woman's National Liberal Union. Her book about the subject, *Woman, Church and the State,* appeared in 1893.

Emma Goldman (1869–1940)
Anarchist, lecturer

AN AVOWED ANARCHIST, EMMA GOLDMAN—OR "Red Emma," as she came to be called—fought for the rights of the individual and believed that organized government led only to abuse of power. Her distrust of authority began early. Growing up in Russia, she saw peasants mistreated by police, experienced persecution for being Jewish, and worked in a glove factory under miserable conditions. She immigrated to America in 1885, but her life as a factory worker in Rochester, New York, was hardly an improvement.

A fiery speaker, Goldman agitated for change, supporting trade unions, birth control, free speech, and resistance to the draft during World War I. She was jailed often and involved in several scandals. In 1892, to support strikers at a steel mill in Homestead, Pennsylvania, Goldman took part in a plot to kill a brutal manager, Henry Clay Frick. The plan failed, and the killer, Alexander Berkman, was sentenced to prison. In 1901 Goldman was accused of participation in the assassination of President William McKinley, but this was never proved. Since she no

> "Anarchism, then, really stands for the liberation of the human mind from the dominion of religion; the liberation of the human body from the dominion of property; liberation from the shackles and restraint of government. Anarchism stands for a social order . . . that will guarantee to every human being free access to the earth and full enjoyment of the necessities of life, according to individual desires, tastes, and inclinations."
>
> EMMA GOLDMAN
> "Anarchism"

longer used violent tactics by then, it is unlikely that she was involved.

By 1919 many Americans believed that a network of dangerous radicals threatened the country, and Goldman was deported for her political views. But she continued to write and speak abroad. Her books include *My Disillusionment with Russia* (1923) about her views on the Russian Revolution, and her autobiography, *Living My Life* (1931).

Maud Gonne (1865–1953)
Irish revolutionary, actress

THE BEAUTIFUL AND charismatic Maud Gonne was a beloved actress as well as a national heroine. The poet W. B. Yeats made no secret of his feelings for her; she inspired many of his love poems and the central character of his play, *The Countess Cathleen* (1892). Gonne's work against the British domination of Ireland began in the 1880s, when she was a speaker for the Land League, fighting for rural tenants' rights against unjust evictions. In 1900, using earnings from her lecture tours,

she formed the Daughters of Ireland, a women's group in support of Irish Independence.

Gonne's husband, John MacBride, played a leading role in the Easter Rising of 1916, and was executed by the British. Afterward she worked to help Irish victims during years of struggle that came to be known as the "Troubles." Although Britain and Ireland came to an agreement with the Anglo-Irish Treaty of 1921, Gonne opposed the settlement because it divided Ireland into two parts and kept the Northern area under British rule. The Women's Prisoners' Defense League, which she founded in 1922, supported Irish Republicans who kept up the struggle against the British.

Gonne remained committed to complete Irish Independence until her death. Her son, Sean MacBride, inherited her love of the country. He was Irish foreign minister from 1948 to 1951 and won the Nobel Peace Prize in 1974.

Olympe de Gouges (1748–1793)
Feminist, writer, activist

O LYMPE DE GOUGES WAS SO FAR AHEAD OF HER time that she had few followers while she was alive. She wanted no less than full equality. When she addressed an all-female audience, urging them to demand the right to serve as warriors and government officials, the women booed and hissed.

Born Marie Gouze in Montauban, France, she rid herself of a lower-class background by inventing an aristocratic father and altering her name to sound more noble. She married and had a son, but after her husband died, she moved to Paris to become a playwright.

In 1789 the French Revolution began. The rebels' slogan, "Liberty, Equality, Fraternity," seemed to support her cause. Encouraged, de Gouges wrote the country's first feminist manifesto. But it soon became clear that women would have no greater equality in the Republic than under the king. Her *Declaration of the Rights of Women* (1791) revised the document by the Marquis de Lafayette and Thomas Jefferson that had sparked the Revolution.

In the end her criticism of the revolutionary leaders and her occasional support of the monarchy caused her downfall. She was found guilty of crimes against the new government and executed by guillotine on November 4, 1793.

Germaine Greer (1939–)
Feminist, writer

I N HER BEST-SELLING BOOK, *THE FEMALE EUNUCH* (1970), the Australian-born feminist Germaine Greer explains that male-oriented society takes away natural female power by training girls to act as if they are inferior to boys. The role of social conditioning on female development is commonly discussed today, attesting to the relevance of Greer's once-controversial ideas.

Greer was not only an academic—she taught at Warwick University—she was also actively involved in the popular culture of 1960s London. She acted on television programs, wrote for countercultural magazines, and avidly followed rock musicians. After the publication of *The Female Eunuch*, she took her feminist message to that most 20th-century medium, television. Striking to look at, witty, and argumentative, she became a popular guest on talk shows. At times Greer was linked with the feminist movement at large, but her individualistic nature always set her apart.

Today Greer is a lecturer at Newnham College, Cambridge University. She has continued to publish. Her book *The Change: Women, Aging, and Menopause* (1991) examines stereotypes of older women.

Sarah Moore Grimké (1792–1873)
Angelina Emily Grimké (1805–1879)
Abolitionists, feminists

S ARAH AND ANGELINA GRIMKÉ PLAYED LEADING roles in the early antislavery and women's rights movements. Although they grew up in a prominent South Carolinian family of slaveholders, they denounced not only their family, but their entire way of life by making a stand.

The Grimké sisters had started to question the morality of slavery as children. Sarah was punished when she was 12 for teaching a slave to read. Both girls were horrified at the brutality they saw inflicted on slaves. As young adults, the sisters moved north to Philadelphia, where, for a time, they joined the Quaker religion. The pivotal moment of their lives came in 1835 when Angelina wrote a letter of support to William Lloyd Garrison, a famed abolitionist. He published the letter in his paper, *The Liberator*, and their careers began. The following year both women published pamphlets condemning slavery and appealing especially to white southern women. While pro-slavery readers reacted with fear, the American Anti-Slavery Society applauded and invited them to speak.

In 1837 the Grimké sisters began lecturing along the East Coast with Theodore Weld. It was shocking at the time that women would speak in public at all, let alone to "mixed crowds" of both sexes, and they endured great criticism for their boldness. Weld and Angelina were married in 1838, and the sisters' touring ceased, but they continued to write. The sisters did much of the research for Weld's book *American Slavery as It Is* (1839), a record of the cruel treatment suffered by slaves.

Clara McBride Hale (1905–1992)
Social welfare worker

CLARA HALE WAS LOVINGLY KNOWN AS "MOTHER Hale," and she acted as a mother to many. Born in Philadelphia, she moved to New York City with her husband, who soon died, leaving her the sole supporter of her family. She worked as a maid briefly but wanted to be with her three children, so she began providing foster care out of her home. In all, she gave 40 foster children happy, stable home lives.

In 1969 Hale's daughter Lorraine saw a drug-addicted mother stumbling and struggling to hold her baby. Lorraine sent the woman to her mother, and within a few months, Hale—who had recently decided to retire—had 22 addicted babies under her care. She founded Hale House, the country's first nonprofit child-care agency, in 1975.

Mother Hale succeeded where others had failed by giving the babies her full attention, holding them through the night as they endured the pain of drug withdrawal. In the 1980s, babies infected with AIDS began to arrive at Hale House. Mother Hale cared for over 1,000 infants before her death. Lorraine Hale is the current president of Hale House.

Fannie Lou Hamer (1917–1977)
Civil rights activist

NEARLY A CENTURY AFTER THE CIVIL WAR HAD won them freedom, many blacks in Mississippi still struggled to survive under conditions that resembled slavery. Working as sharecroppers for white plantation owners, they received very little pay and were forced to live in miserable housing. Fannie Lou Hamer had been a sharecropper for almost 40 years when her life took a dramatic turn.

In 1962 representatives of the Southern Christian Leadership Conference and the Student Nonviolent Coordinating Committee visited her town, urging blacks to register to vote. It took courage to make that stand. When Hamer registered, she lost her job and home, and she continually received threats. After one protest, she was arrested and beaten, leaving her eye and kidneys permanently damaged. But Hamer didn't give up.

In 1964 she helped found the Mississippi Freedom Democratic party. The MFDP put pressure on the state's Democratic party to give black citizens political representation.

Hamer believed it was important to help needy blacks support themselves, rather than rely on federal

antipoverty programs. She started the Freedom Farm Cooperative, where people could grow their own food and opened a garment factory to provide jobs. She also helped start a day-care center and raised funds for housing. By the end of her life, Hamer, who had only six years of schooling, held many honorary degrees from universities acknowledging her important work in the fight for civil rights.

Lydia Sayer Hasbrouck (1827–1910)
Clothing reformer, radical, editor

LYDIA HASBROUCK WAS WEARING "BLOOMERS" (pantaloons covered by a knee-length skirt) well before their namesake, Amelia Bloomer, discovered them. It was 1849 when she abandoned her ladylike but constricting long skirts and adopted the comfortable outfit. As a result, she was barred from attending the Seward Seminary. The incident inspired her to activism. She soon made a name for herself as a lecturer on dress reform.

In 1856 the publisher John W. Hasbrouck, invited Lydia to Middletown, New York, to edit a new journal, *The Sibyl.* They were married a few months later—and the bride wore white bloomers. For eight years, the paper was a forum for Hasbrouck's ideas. In addition to dress reform, she supported temperance, opposed tobacco use, and advocated a healthful diet and exercise. She was also an ardent suffragist, at one point refusing to pay taxes since she could not vote. In response, the tax collector stole a pair of her bloomers to auction off.

Hasbrouck was elected to Middletown's school board in 1880, in the first state election in which women were allowed to participate. Unlike almost all other women reformers of her era, she continued to wear bloomers for the rest of her life.

Le Ly Hayslip (1945–)
Humanitarian, autobiographer

IN 1987 LE LY HAYSLIP, A SURVIVOR OF THE horrors of the Vietnam War, created the East Meets West Foundation to provide much-needed humanitarian relief in her homeland. Among other projects, the Foundation has opened a clinic for homeless children in Hayslip's native village of Ky La and built a medical facility at China Beach. She encourages American veterans of the war to participate in the work, too, and to confront their anger and guilt constructively.

In her book, *When Heaven and Earth Changed Places* (1989), Hayslip describes how, as a girl during the war, she helped the Viet Cong in their fight for independence—like many villagers—digging tunnels or serving as a lookout. Often the enemy, the American and South Vietnamese soldiers, forced villagers to work, too. This was a doubly dangerous situation. If the enemy caught them helping their people, the villagers could be tortured or killed. But they might also receive the same treatment from the Viet Cong, who considered submission to the enemy betrayal.

After the war Hayslip endured terrible poverty and a series of unhappy relationships, but she made her way to America and became a successful businesswoman. In 1993 she wrote a second memoir, *Child of War, Woman of Peace.* That same year, Oliver Stone released the movie *Heaven and Earth,* which is based on her life.

Dorothy Irene Height (1912–)
Civil rights and women's rights activist

DOROTHY IRENE HEIGHT RETIRED AS PRESIDENT of the National Council of Negro Women in January 1998, after serving for 40 years. She had been hand-picked for the job by the Council's founder, Mary McLeod Bethune, who met her when she accompanied Eleanor Roosevelt to an NCNW meeting.

A proven leader, Height was president of the Pennsylvania State Federation of Girls Clubs by age 14. A member of the United Christian Youth movement, she attended conferences in America and abroad during the 1930s. In 1938 she helped Eleanor Roosevelt plan the World Youth

Congress and began working with the Young Christian Women's Association. Among her accomplishments was the complete desegregation of YWCA facilities. As national president of the Delta Sigma Theta sorority from 1947 to 1953, she worked to improve job opportunities for black women. She expanded the scope of the group as well, encouraging members to work in needy communities around the world.

After becoming president of the NCNW in 1957, Height improved and initiated a variety of programs. In the 1960s she was not only a strong presence during the critical years of civil rights unrest in the South, but she also traveled to Africa to draw attention to social conditions there. In 1986 she established the annual Black Family Reunion, to honor African American families.

Alice Henry (1857–1943)
Journalist, suffragist, social reformer

AUSTRALIAN-BORN ALICE HENRY WORKED AS A journalist and social reformer in her homeland and the United States. She made her mark as a feminist trade union advocate in particular, arguing that female workers were more easily exploited and therefore in special need of the organized power of unions. Henry also called for protective legislation for female workers and brought an international sensibility to the issue.

Henry began her journalism career in 1884, writing for the *Melbourne Argus* and the *Australasian*. Her broad reform interests gradually focused after she moved to the United States in 1906 and became involved with Jane Addams's Hull House in Chicago. In 1911 Henry became the editor of *Life and Labor*, a monthly magazine published by the National Women's Trade Union League. Her books, *The Trade Union Woman* (1915) and *Woman and the Labor Movement* (1923), were important works, both as documentation of women's trade union history and for the promotion of social reform.

After traveling and speaking in the United States, Europe, and Australia, Henry settled in her native land. She devoted the end of her career to promoting medical and educational programs for Australians living in rural areas.

Octavia Hill (1838–1912)
Housing reformer, social worker

DURING HER LIFETIME, OCTAVIA HILL WAS FAMED as a social worker whose goal was to improve the quality of life for England's urban poor. Today she is remembered more for her efforts to preserve the environment. Hill shared a common Victorian idea, that beautiful surroundings had a "civilizing" effect on people who otherwise experienced only the dreary ugliness of the industrial inner city.

In 1864 Hill and John Ruskin, an art critic, bought three apartment houses in the London slums. Hill was an active landlord. She even performed some of the necessary cleaning and repair work herself to prepare the buildings for tenants. Believing that personal contact was beneficial, she held weekly teas where rent was collected in a friendly, social setting.

In 1875 Hill formed the Kyrle Society to plant city gardens and bring art and music to the slums. The Open Spaces Division of the Society worked to preserve London's remaining green areas and led to the formation of the National Trust in 1895. The Trust, which is still active, protects natural and historic properties by purchasing the land and helping to maintain it.

Hill also resolved to combat air pollution, which had become a serious problem, because coal was the most common fuel at the time. In 1881 she organized an exhibition to inform the public about alternative fuels, and founded the Coal Smoke Abatement Society in 1898. As a result of Hill's efforts, the air quality was dramatically improved.

Hiratsuka Raicho (1886–1971)
Feminist

"In the beginning, woman was the sun." This first line of Hiratsuka Raicho's poem became the motto for her women's literary magazine, *Seito* (Bluestocking), founded in 1911. She was making a reference to the all-powerful sun goddess, Amaterasu, from whom it was believed all Japanese emperors descended. Many women's groups in Japan were moved by the phrase, and it became a common feminist rallying cry.

In addition to *Seito*, Hiratsuka founded *Seitosha*, or the Bluestocking Society. Strongly influenced by Western culture, these women were outspoken and independent—their type soon came to be called the New Woman. In 1920 she formed the New Women's Association with fellow feminist Ichikawa Fusae and others. Within two years, they helped bring about the revision of the Peace Preservation Laws, removing some restrictions on women's political participation.

Remaining active in many causes until her death, Hiratsuka founded an all-female consumers' union in 1929 and, in the 1950s, led the Federation of Japanese Women's Associations. A committed pacifist, she helped to organize the World Mothers' Convention in 1954 as part of her campaign against the hydrogen bomb.

Hortensia (1st century B.C.E.)
Women's rights advocate

The idea of protesting "taxation without representation" is not new. Hortensia used this argument over 2,000 years ago, in 43 B.C.E. The assassination of Julius Caesar had sparked a civil war in Rome, and the Second Triumvirate, or ruling commission, decided to tax 1,400 of the city's richest women to pay for it. First the women appealed to female family members of the triumvirs, Mark Antony, Octavian, and Lepidus. But Antony's wife, Fulvia, treated them rudely, so they forced their way into the men's meeting.

Hortensia argued that since women did not hold political office and had nothing to do with the war, they should not be taxed. "Why should we share the penalties if we have no part in the wrongdoing?" she asked. She emphasized, however, that they would willingly support a war against an outside enemy.

At first the men reacted with anger, but Hortensia's argument was persuasive, and the crowd outside supported her. The next day it was announced that only the 400 wealthiest women would be taxed. Hortensia's speech was admired and studied for years afterward.

Dolores Huerta (1930–)
Labor leader

Growing up in Stockton, California, Huerta was familiar with the poor laborers who came to town during harvest season, traveling from farm to farm in search of a job. She knew that their working conditions were often terrible. Her father, a Mexican immigrant, was a migrant laborer and political activist, and she revered his example.

Huerta worked for several years with the Mexican American community. Then, in 1962, she joined with César Chávez to concentrate on issues faced by farmworkers. Their group, the Farm Workers Association, grew into the powerful United Farm Workers. Huerta

devised strategies and led picket lines during strikes, encouraging workers to quit working to force employers to listen. She was known for driving a hard bargain in negotiations. In 1968 she tried out the tactic of boycotting, asking consumers not to buy table grapes until farmers listened to their workers' demands. By 1970 new worker contracts were being negotiated.

Huerta went on to promote boycotts of lettuce, grapes, and wine. Her work led to the passage of the Agricultural Labor Relations Act of 1975. She has paid a high price for her leadership; she was often away from her 11 children. In 1988 she was beaten so badly by police at a nonviolent protest that she needed surgery. As soon as she recovered, though, she resumed her activism. Dolores Huerta has shown that nonviolent methods can bring about social change.

Anne Hutchinson (1591–1643)
Puritan, religious leader

LIKE MANY COLONISTS, ANNE HUTCHINSON AND her family left England to seek religious freedom in the New World. Settling in the Puritan Massachusetts Bay Colony in 1634, Hutchinson soon became a respected midwife. She also invited people to her home for informal religious meetings. There she discussed the sermons of her minister, John Cotton, as well as her own religious ideas. Hutchinson spoke fervently and well; many people came to listen.

Hutchinson criticized the "Covenant of Works," the idea that a person had to perform certain deeds during life in order to achieve salvation. Instead, she believed in a "Covenant of Grace." She thought that the only way to get to heaven was by having true faith in God. However, the powerful clergy of the colony believed in the Covenant of Works.

In 1637 John Winthrop, one of Hutchinson's most determined opponents, became governor. He and his followers accused her of being a traitor and brought her to trial. Mocked for daring to think that women could preach and betrayed by many who had

> **"I thinke the soule to be nothing but Light."**
>
> ANNE HUTCHINSON
> **At her trial in 1637**

supported her earlier, Hutchinson was found guilty and banished from the colony. Five years later, she was living in the New Netherlands colony when the settlement was attacked by Indians, and she was killed.

Ichikawa Fusae (1893–1981)
Politician, suffragist, feminist

ICHIKAWA FUSAE NOT ONLY LED JAPAN'S FLEDGLING feminist movement, but after the country allowed women the vote in 1945, she held political office for many years. Starting as a teacher in a village school, she challenged her country's idea of women's proper role with each successive job. She became a clerk for a stockbroker, the first woman to write for the newspaper *Nagoya Shimbun*, and a labor organizer.

In 1920 Ichikawa cofounded the New Women's Association to campaign for expanded political rights for women. Continuing her work as a labor reformer, she led a women's group for the International Labour Organization. She cofounded the Women's Suffrage League in 1924 and, when their goal was achieved, she established Japan's League of Women Voters to educate women about how to use their newly granted rights.

From 1952 to 1970, Ichikawa served in the Japanese Diet, or parliament. After a brief absence, she was returned to her office in 1974 and in 1980, winning both elections by a landslide. She distinguished herself as an honest politician who fought against government corruption and donated her pay raises to women's groups.

Patricia Ireland (1945–)
Lawyer, activist

IN THE 1970S PATRICIA Ireland, a flight attendant for Pan Am Airlines, discovered that her health insurance did not cover her husband. Male airline employees' spouses, on the other hand, received full health benefits. Looking for a way to assert her rights,

Ireland found out that the National Organization for Women offers legal help in such cases. So with NOW's help, she launched a successful lawsuit against her employer.

Inspired by that experience, Ireland began to study law. After earning her degree in 1975, Ireland often worked with NOW on a *pro bono* basis, volunteering her services for cases like the one she had initiated. She also stepped into the spotlight in the abortion debate, defending women's right to have a safe, legal way to end pregnancy.

NOW president Molly Yard resigned because of poor health in 1991, and Ireland, by then vice-president, took her place. That was a busy year for NOW. Membership increased as women across the nation followed congressional hearings in which Anita Hill charged Supreme Court nominee Clarence Thomas with sexual harassment. Ireland's soft-spoken demeanor and her calm handling of such issues—she remains president of NOW—have done much to establish the organization as a political entity rather than a fringe group.

Helen Hunt Jackson (1830–1885)
Native American rights activist, writer

Helen Hunt Jackson grew up in Amherst, Massachusetts, and was a lifelong friend of the poet Emily Dickinson. Her first marriage to the army engineer Edward Hunt ended in tragedy. One of their children died in 1854, Edward was killed in an accident in 1863, and Helen's remaining son died of diphtheria in 1865. She began writing poetry to ease her grief. Although she was an immediate success as a writer, Helen disliked publicity and usually wrote under false names.

In 1875 Helen married a wealthy banker named William Jackson and moved to Colorado Springs, Colorado. Gradually, she became aware of the troubles the Native Americans who lived nearby faced. She heard the Tonca chief, Standing Bear, give a speech in 1879, and soon committed herself to the Indian rights cause. Her book, *A Century of Dishonor* (1881), documented in detail the government's massacres and forced relocation of Indian tribes. This led to a government-appointed position investigating the treatment of the Mission

Indians in California. Perhaps most effective of all was her novel *Ramona* (1884), which romanticized the issue and aroused widespread public sympathy. Although it cannot be said that Jackson's work led to immediate changes in governmental policy, she did much to raise public awareness of the sufferings of Native Americans.

Aletta Jacobs (1854–1929)
Suffragist, physician

Determined to go to medical school even though no university accepted women, Aletta Jacobs wrote to the Prime Minister of the Netherlands asking him to force a school to admit her. He wrote back, saying that, as long as her father agreed, he would arrange it. Luckily, Jacobs's father—a doctor himself—honored his daughter's intelligence. She graduated in 1878 from the University of Groningen, becoming Holland's first female doctor.

Ignoring the bitter disapproval of her colleagues, she joined her father's practice and also began to provide medical care for the poor. In 1882 she again proved herself a pioneer, establishing the world's first birth control clinic in Amsterdam. Again the medical community opposed her actions. The conflict lasted over three decades. But her resolve never weakened, and the clinic remained open.

A champion of women's rights, including labor issues, pacifism, and suffrage, Jacobs worked on national and international levels. She collaborated with Carrie Catt and Jane Addams. Women in the Netherlands won the vote in 1919. After that, Jacobs began to work for Asian women's rights.

Fatima Jinnah (1893–1967)
Women's rights activist, politician

BORN IN KARACHI, PAKISTAN, FATIMA JINNAH played an important role in the campaign led by her older brother, Ali Jinnah, to create a Muslim country that was independent of the predominantly Hindu India. Fatima's particular goal was to improve the status of Muslim women—among conservative members of the religion, women have little social standing. Focusing on broadening and modernizing her countrymen's orthodox views, she joined the Muslim League in 1934 and became leader of the All-India Muslim Women's Committee in 1938. She also founded a women's medical college in Lahore.

England liberated its Indian colony in 1947, and Ali Jinnah became the first Governor General of Pakistan. When he died the next year, Fatima withdrew from public life. However, General Mohammed Ayub Khan's totalitarian regime in East Pakistan (now Bangladesh) so disturbed her that she came out of retirement in 1954. She even challenged Khan in the 1965 presidential election. Although she lost, Fatima Jinnah remained a beloved public figure and was known as "Madar-i-Millat" (Mother of the Country).

Joan of Arc (1412–1431)
Religious and military leader

IN 1429 THE FRENCH WERE HOPELESSLY ENTANGLED with English invaders in what is now known as the Hundred Years' War. France's ruling family, too divided to provide leadership, did not even crown a new king after the death of Charles VI. Territory had been lost, and many people had been killed. Then an uneducated peasant girl named Joan of Arc stepped forward to restore the nation's pride.

A devout Catholic, Joan believed the saints communicated with her directly, telling her to dress as a warrior and lead her people to victory. In 1429 she visited the Dauphin (the heir to France's throne) and convinced him to support her. The 16-year-old girl received troops and the rank of captain. Unflinchingly, she led her army to victory at Orléans in May 1429 and went on to take other English strongholds, persuading the Dauphin to hold his coronation in July.

Finally, in 1430, Joan was captured by King Charles's enemies and accused of many crimes, including wearing men's clothes and claiming to speak directly with God. On May 30, 1431, after enduring a hard trial, she was burned at the stake. Although he had not helped her when she most needed it, the king reversed her death sentence 25 years later. In 1920 Joan of Arc—also known as *La Pucelle*, or the Maid of Orléans—was declared a saint.

Mary Harris Jones (1830–1930)
Labor leader

IRISH-BORN MOTHER JONES WAS NO STRANGER TO hardship and loneliness. In 1867 she lost her husband and four children to a yellow fever epidemic in Memphis, Tennessee. She lost her home

Mother Jones on her 100th birthday

and her dressmaking business to Chicago's Great Fire of 1871. Starting over with only the clothes on her back, she sought refuge in a church and began to recruit workers for the Knights of Labor, which met nearby. For the rest of her life, she kept no permanent address, choosing instead to live among the workers she inspired.

Jones fought tirelessly for workers' rights. She took up the causes of railroad and textile mill workers, among others, but was most famous for her association with American miners, beginning with the strikes of 1891. Often arrested and barred from meeting halls, Jones would speak in the street. She encouraged workers to demand better wages, shorter work hours, and the right to organize unions.

Union officials appreciated her help, but her inflammatory tactics worried them. Wearing her proper long dress and bonnet, she would stand in front of armed guards and dare them to shoot at her. Violence often erupted between workers and their bosses when she appeared.

For decades Jones participated in major strikes at West Virginia and Colorado mines. Even when she was 82, Jones still posed such a threat that Colorado officials tried to physically remove her from the state. Mother Jones, "the miner's angel," lived to be 100, and received congratulations from around the nation on her birthday, celebrated seven months before her death.

Helen Joseph (1905–1992)
Antiapartheid activist

HELEN JOSEPH DIDN'T START OUT AS A POLITICAL radical. Born and educated in England, she lived in India after graduating from college, then went to South Africa in 1931. There she married a dentist and socialized with other white middle-class housewives. During World War II, however, she volunteered to teach current events to British air force women, and her eyes were opened to the injustice of apartheid. Joseph began to work with the activist Solly Sachs, and by the mid-1950s, she had emerged as a leader. She was a founder of the Congress of Democrats, a white party that supported the black African National Congress. She worked for the Federation of South African Women, and organized demonstrations in the capital of Pretoria.

The government's response to protest was harsh. In 1956 Joseph was arrested for high treason. From then on, she was repeatedly banned from public activity and imprisoned. She lived under house arrest for nine years. Despite the threat of violence, Joseph held secret meetings to continue the fight. In her autobiography, *Side by Side* (1985), she expressed optimism that her side would win—sooner rather than later. And, in fact, she did live to see her country's first steps toward integration.

Apartheid

Racial segregation was nothing new in South Africa after the Dutch and then the British settled there. But, after the National Party came to power in 1948, they instituted an official policy called *apartheid*, or "apartness." A series of laws were enacted, classifying people by race, specifying areas in which they could live and work, refusing political rights to nonwhites and requiring them to carry passes. Gradually, because of international criticism and internal protest, the tide started to turn. In 1990 President F. W. de Klerk began repealing laws that upheld apartheid. Nelson Mandela was elected president in 1994, and many other blacks entered government posts that year.

Helen Adams Keller (1880–1968)

Advocate for the disabled, writer

As SHE APPROACHED THE AGE OF TWO, WHEN most children are learning to use language, Helen Keller lost her hearing and sight as the result of an illness. Her parents wanted desperately to help, but the little girl was increasingly difficult to handle. She often expressed her frustration by lashing out with her fists. At last, in 1887, the Kellers brought the teacher Anne Sullivan to live at their Alabama home. Sullivan, an orphan, had been almost blind as a child—her sight had been improved by surgery—so she understood the isolation Keller faced.

Within a month Sullivan succeeded in taming Keller and conveying the idea of language to her. A whole new world opened up as the seven-year-old girl realized the connection between an object and its name, which Sullivan spelled into her open hand using special sign language. She quickly learned hundreds of words. Always working with "Teacher," Keller went on to master Braille, an alphabet composed of tiny raised bumps on paper; to understand speech by touching a speaking person's lips; and, to a lesser degree, to speak herself. In 1904 she graduated *cum laude* (with honors) from Radcliffe College in Massachusetts.

For the remainder of her life, Keller was a highly visible public figure. She lectured widely and published several books, including *The Story of My Life* (1902), *The World I Live In* (1909), and *Teacher: Anne Sullivan Macy* (1955). Her efforts were instrumental in securing private and government assistance for the disabled.

Florence Kelley (1859–1932)

Social reformer, children's rights advocate, labor lawyer

IN 1891 FLORENCE KELLEY, A RESIDENT OF JANE Addams's Hull House in Chicago, discovered that many factories paid their employees—primarily women and children—very little money and kept them at work for ten or more hours a day in dark, cramped rooms. Kelley, a Socialist dedicated to advancing workers' rights, conducted a thorough investigation and took her findings to the Illinois legislature. To be even more effective, she resumed her law studies, begun in Switzerland several years before, and was admitted to the Illinois bar in 1894. Her efforts led to new state laws banning child labor and limiting the work day for women.

In 1899 Kelley became secretary of the National Consumers' League and led consumer boycotts to protest unfair treatment of workers. She had learned this strategy as a child growing up in Philadelphia, where her relative Sarah Pugh, an abolitionist Quaker, had refused to purchase any products that had been made by slave labor. Kelley went on to become a founder of the New York and then the National Child Labor Committees and the Federal Children's Bureau. Her successes in labor reform helped to impose federal restrictions on child labor, the length of work days, and the minimum wage.

Ellen Key (1849–1926)

Feminist, writer

ELLEN KEY WAS BORN IN SUNDSHOLM, SWEDEN, but moved to Stockholm when her father was elected to government office. Already concerned with social issues, Key had started a library back in her hometown, and she wrote for the journal *Idun* in the city. She became truly active in social reform after a family financial crisis forced her to earn a living as a teacher, lecturer, and writer. During the last two decades of the 19th century, her essays concerning property rights of women, social reform, and family life were both influential and controversial. From 1903 to 1909, she made lecture tours throughout Europe. Her book, *The Century of the Child* (1909), assured her a place in the international spotlight.

Over the course of her career, Key wrote 30 books. Many people thought her ideas were too radical, especially those concerning love and marriage. However, while she encouraged single women to work in the public sphere, she always stressed that married women should stay at home with their children. She considered motherhood the most noble calling, a way to promote peace and shape the future for the good of all.

Coretta Scott King (1927–)
Civil rights activist

O N APRIL 4, 1968, DR. Martin Luther King, Jr. was assassinated in Memphis, Tennessee. In spite of the violence of his death and her grief at losing her beloved husband, Coretta Scott King held firm to the couple's shared belief in the power of nonviolence. She continued to call for a peaceful stance from Dr. King's supporters, many of whom were on the verge of rioting.

The Kings, both southerners, met in Boston. Coretta, an excellent student who had graduated first in her Alabama high school class, was studying voice at the New England Conservatory of Music. Martin Luther King was working on his Ph.D. in philosophy at Boston University. They married in 1953 and moved to Alabama after graduating. His successful leadership of the Montgomery bus boycott in 1955 catapulted Dr. King into national prominence.

Coretta participated in civil rights activities near home and abroad, while raising their four children and pursuing her career in music. She performed a series of "freedom concerts." When her husband had scheduling conflicts, she often spoke in his place.

Since the assassination, Coretta Scott King has been involved in many reform issues, such as women's rights, nuclear weapons policy, and the anti-apartheid movement. As a memorial to her husband, she created a complex in Atlanta, Georgia, that includes a museum, a library, research facilities, and the King Center for Nonviolent Social Change.

Beate Klarsfeld (1939–)
Anti-Nazi activist

B EATE KUNZEL, THE DAUGHTER OF A GERMAN soldier, grew up knowing little about her father's activities during World War II. It was not until she went to study in Paris and fell in love with Serge Klarsfeld, whose father had died at Auschwitz, that she understood that Hitler had intended to exterminate the Jews. After marrying in 1963, Beate and Serge began to learn all they could about the Holocaust.

The Klarsfelds were horrified when Kurt Kiesinger, a former Nazi, was elected Chancellor of West Germany in 1967. Beate wrote articles about his past, but she couldn't reach enough people. Frustrated, she took a more dramatic approach. One night in 1968, while Kiesinger was giving a speech, Beate ran up to the podium and slapped him. This sort of public confrontation would become a central part of the Klarsfelds' tactics.

At last the media was interested. Beate and Serge were ready with stacks of documents to prove their case. Kiesinger was not reelected. Since then, the Klarsfelds have pursued many former Nazis, most famously Klaus Barbie. They have received prison sentences and death threats, but Beate is determined to punish the crimes committed by her parents' generation.

Aleksandra Mikhaylovna Kollontay (1872–1952)
Revolutionary, women's rights activist

A LEKSANDRA KOLLONTAY, THE DAUGHTER OF AN Imperial Russian Army general and the wife of an army officer, belonged to a privileged social group. She left that comfortable life to become a Socialist revolutionary. After 1908 she was exiled from Russia for her political beliefs, so she traveled in Europe and America, speaking out for women's liberation within the context of a worker's revolution. Kollontay was a member of the Bolshevik party, which overthrew the Russian monarchy in the October Revolution of 1917.

Returning home—to a country renamed the Soviet Union—Kollontay was appointed to many high posts, but this new government also found her outspokenness difficult. She advocated reform in marriage and divorce laws, women's legal rights, and child care. Most controversially, she joined the Workers' Opposition group in calling for greater democratization within the Communist party. As a result, she was repeatedly sent on diplomatic assignments to other countries to keep her out of the way.

During the 1920s, Kollontay served as minister to Norway and Mexico. Posted in Sweden after 1930, she played a major role in negotiating the 1944 peace between the Soviet Union and Finland during World War II.

Margaret E. Kuhn (1905–1995)
Social activist

As PROGRAMS COORDINATOR FOR THE UNITED Presbyterian Church in New York City, Maggie Kuhn had long worked for social justice. But she had never experienced discrimination herself—until she was forced to retire just because she was 65. In 1971 she and five other elders joined a group of

youth protesting the Vietnam War. Soon, the media tagged them the "Gray Panthers," a catchy reference to the Black Panther party, a militant African American group of the same era. The Gray Panthers were not militant, but they were insistent. Under Kuhn's leadership they grew into a national organization.

Working at local, state, and national levels, they have fought for social security benefits and more liberal retirement laws, as well as general political issues. They reject media stereotypes of the elderly as weak or ineffectual. Kuhn always emphasized the importance of young and old people working together to learn how much they have in common. Her autobiography is entitled *No Stone Unturned* (1991).

Susette La Flesche Tibbles (1854–1903)
Native American rights advocate

Susette La Flesche, BETTER KNOWN BY HER translated Omaha name, "Bright Eyes," was born on the Nebraska Omaha reservation. Her father, the Omaha chief, wanted his children to be familiar with European American as well as Native American culture, so he sent them to a Presbyterian school. Eventually, Bright Eyes's brother, Francis, became an ethnologist; her sister, Susan, became a physician; Susette became a teacher and returned to work at the reservation.

In 1877 the Ponca Indians, another Nebraska tribe, were forced off their land by the federal government and sent to Oklahoma, where a third of them died from disease. Their chief, Standing Bear, tried to lead a group back to his homeland, but they were arrested. Bright Eyes, her father, and the editor of the *Omaha Herald*, Thomas H. Tibbles, came to their aid, and the Poncas were freed.

After that, Thomas Tibbles arranged a lecture tour to publicize the plight of the American Indian. Bright Eyes, her brother and sister, and Standing Bear traveled in America and abroad, speaking out against the forced displacement of Native Americans. Of the group, Bright Eyes received particular attention for her persuasive speeches and charismatic presence. In 1881 she married Tibbles and went on to write stories and articles in support of her cause.

Julia Clifford Lathrop (1858–1932)
Social worker, reformer

JULIA LATHROP'S FRIEND JANE ADDAMS CALLED her "one of the most useful women in the country." A native of Rockford, Illinois, Lathrop began her long reform career in 1893 when she was appointed to the Illinois Board of Charities. The fact that she personally investigated all 102 charitable institutions in the state and wrote detailed suggestions for their improvement demonstrates her commitment to the needy. She was especially dedicated to child welfare and improving treatment of the mentally ill.

Lathrop lived at Addams's Hull House in Chicago for 20 years. She worked with fellow resident Florence Kelley on labor issues and with Sophonisba Breckenbridge in the social work department of the University of Chicago. In 1912 President William Taft appointed her director of the Children's Bureau of the Department of Commerce and Labor. She was soon respected worldwide as a children's rights advocate.

Although ill health forced Lathrop to resign from her federal post in 1921, she stayed busy. She led the Illinois League of Women Voters from 1922 to 1924 and dedicated the last seven years of her life to the Child Welfare Committee of the League of Nations.

Ann Lee (1736–1784)
Religious leader

ANN LEE BELONGED TO AN OFFSHOOT OF THE Society of Friends that was known as the Shaking Quakers because believers curiously swayed with fervor during religious services. Lee had married only reluctantly in 1762, and after all four of her babies died, she concluded that she had been punished by God. She performed rigorous penance and eventually experienced a vision convincing her that marriage was against God's law and that she should be celibate.

Lee began preaching in the streets of her native Manchester, England. Hostile crowds often threw stones and threatened her. In 1770 church authorities, who frowned on all Quaker and Shaker activities, imprisoned her.

In 1774 Lee and a few followers sailed to America and established a religious community in Watervliet near Albany, New York. They stressed pacifism, common property, and equality of sex, race, and class. The idea attracted followers, although, as always, their beliefs were controversial. Patriots considered pacifism to be treason, so Lee was imprisoned again in 1780.

Lee's followers called her "Mother Ann" or "Ann the Way." They believed she was the female half of Christ. The American Shaker sect continued to grow even after her death, reaching its peak of popularity in the early 19th century.

Belva Ann Bennett Lockwood (1830–1917)
Equal rights activist, lawyer

AS A TEACHER, BELVA LOCKWOOD WAS OUTRAGED to learn that the men working at her school earned twice as much as she did for doing the same job. Lockwood was determined to change all that. She returned to college to earn her degree and in 1867 opened one of the first coeducational schools in Washington, D.C. Then, while her husband ran the school, she set about becoming a lawyer.

Three universities denied her application—what would a woman, especially a married woman, do with a law degree? Finally she was admitted to the National University Law School. While there, Lockwood wrote a bill calling for female government employees to receive equal pay for equal work. It passed into law in 1872.

Although Lockwood was admitted to the District of Columbia bar, the U.S. Court of Claims refused to let her plead cases. Lockwood single-handedly pushed the necessary legislation through Congress and became the first woman to plead a case before the Supreme Court in 1879.

In addition to her successful law practice, Lockwood campaigned for women's rights. She lectured, worked with both the National and the American Woman Suffrage Associations, and even ran for president of the United States in 1884 and 1888. During the 1890s and beyond, she worked for peace, holding office in organizations such as the Universal Peace Union and the Nobel Peace Prize nominating committee.

Juliette Gordon Low (1860–1927)
Founder of the Girl Scouts of America

JULIETTE GORDON, KNOWN TO HER FRIENDS AS Daisy, was a privileged member of Savannah, Georgia, society. After attending private boarding schools, she often traveled in Europe. She married the rich English playboy William Low in 1886, and the couple socialized with the Prince of Wales. She was even presented to Queen Victoria. In 1902 William died, leaving her independently wealthy and eager to find an outlet for her natural energy and spirit of leadership.

In 1911 Low met the English military hero Sir Robert Baden-Powell. He had founded the British Boy Scouts, and by then there was also a sister group, the Girl Guides. The idea of introducing young people to the outdoors while teaching them citizenship and social skills appealed to Low, who had been quite athletic as a girl. The next year, she took the idea home to Savannah.

Low's first troop of 16 girls camped, played sports, and wore tidy uniforms. Girls all over town clamored to join. In 1915 Low founded a national organization, the Girl Scouts of America. She served as president until 1920 and remained involved with the Scouts for the rest of her life. Today the Girl Scouts has more than 2.5 million members.

Rosa Luxemburg (1870?–1919)
Revolutionary, labor reform leader

ROSA LUXEMBURG WAS BORN TO JEWISH PARENTS in Russian-controlled Poland. At age 11 she witnessed a pogrom—an attack by Russians and Poles against the Jews. In high school Luxemburg began to read Karl Marx, who advocated socialism, a political system in which all property is owned and controlled by the people. Her liberal politics forced her to flee to

Zurich, Switzerland, in 1889. While there, she earned a doctorate in law and political science. Along with a colleague, Leo Jogiches, she founded the Polish Social Democratic party in 1894.

In 1905 Luxemburg returned to Poland to organize workers' revolts and was arrested. The pamphlet she wrote afterward, *The Mass Strike*, expressed the vast scope of her revolutionary hopes. She called for laborers worldwide to join together in one gigantic strike, seizing control from their oppressors.

Luxemburg opposed World War I, because she did not believe that nations should fight one another. She spent most of the war in prison, where she formed the Socialist Spartacus League with Karl Liebknecht. In early 1919 Luxemburg and Liebknecht were arrested while taking part in an uprising. They were tortured and then murdered by German soldiers. Luxemburg's ambitious dream of uniting the world to end tyranny remains far from being realized, but her ideas are still admired by many political activists.

Mary Mason Lyon (1797–1849)
Educator

MARY LYON FIRST STARTED TEACHING AT THE AGE of 17, and went on to work and study at a number of Massachusetts schools. She was particularly influenced by the founder of the Byfield Female Seminary, Reverend Joseph Emerson, who believed women should receive a solid education, not devote their time to leisure activities like music and dancing. Using ideas inspired by Emerson, Lyon went on to participate in the creation of three schools between 1823 and 1828.

Lyon wanted to reach as many women as possible—and to provide them with a solid college education. At the time, only Oberlin College in Ohio accepted female students. So in 1834 she began to raise funds for a permanently endowed women's boarding college. In order to serve middle-class students as well as wealthy ones, she decided that everyone would share domestic chores, and she kept the teachers' salaries to a minimum.

The Mount Holyoke Female Seminary opened its doors in 1837, teaching the same subjects and using the same texts that men used. Under Lyon's visionary leadership, the college produced highly qualified graduates, most of whom became teachers or missionaries. Now called Mount Holyoke College, the school continues to provide an outstanding higher education for women.

Aimee Semple McPherson (1890–1944)
Evangelist

IN 1923 AIMEE SEMPLE MCPHERSON OPENED her Angelus Temple, or "Church of the Foursquare Gospel," in Los Angeles. After years of traveling around the country to preach, she finally had a permanent pulpit, and she took advantage of it, staging revival meetings that were as much spectacle as sermon. The 5,000-seat building was often filled to capacity. A gifted speaker and a dramatic presence, McPherson preached every night, dressed in a white robe and a blue cape. She presented faith healings, adult baptisms, pageants, and music by a 50-piece band. Her radio station broadcast the event to the whole city of Los Angeles.

Religion played a very important role in McPherson's life from the beginning. As a child, she accompanied her mother in work for the Salvation Army. At age 18, she married a Pentecostal preacher, Robert Semple, and was ordained as a preacher herself. After Robert's death in China, where they were working as missionaries, Aimee returned to America. Her second marriage, to Harold S. McPherson, ended

in 1921, partly because of Aimee's growing dedication to preaching.

McPherson's sermons were not the only part of her life that was dramatic. She caused a sensation in 1926 when she disappeared for weeks and then reappeared just as suddenly, claiming she had been kidnapped. She was involved in numerous lawsuits over shaky finances. A scandalous marriage and family quarrels also made the news. Her death in 1944 from an overdose of sleeping pills was ruled accidental. Through it all, her church remained popular, and her son assumed leadership after she died.

Winnie Madikizela-Mandela (1934?–)
Antiapartheid activist, social worker

WINNIE MADIKIZELA, THE FIRST BLACK MEDICAL social worker in South Africa, was 24 when she married Nelson Mandela, leader of the African National Congress. Together they worked to end apartheid, the South African system of segregation and discrimination against blacks.

Accused of treason, Nelson Mandela was imprisoned in 1962, and Winnie had to carry on alone. She was regularly harassed by the government but continued to do social work and speak out for freedom, becoming known as the "Mother of the Nation." Eventually, though, there were signs that she may have used ruthless tactics to promote her cause. In 1988 she was associated with the kidnapping of four black youths whom she believed were police informants. One of the boys had been murdered. When the case came to trial in 1991, Winnie's bodyguard was found guilty of murder, and she was convicted for participating in the crimes.

Nelson Mandela was released in 1990, and he continued to work with Winnie for a time. She was elected president of the ANC Women's League in 1993. The next year, Nelson became president of South Africa's first multiracial government, and he gave her a cabinet post. But the controversy surrounding his wife became too great. Nelson removed Winnie from her position shortly before divorcing her in 1996. She continues to seek a role in South African politics.

Rigoberta Menchú (1959–)
Indigenous rights activist

RIGOBERTA MENCHÚ'S PEOPLE, THE QUICHÉ Mayan Indians, have always lived in Guatemala and make up a majority of the population, but they have been persecuted by the country's military government for over 30 years. Menchú has witnessed this brutality firsthand. Her father, Vicente Menchú, became involved in the peasants' fight for political rights, attracting the attention of the security forces. In 1979 and 1980, Menchú's brother, father, and mother were murdered, one after the other.

Menchú escaped to Mexico in 1981 and became an activist for Indian rights in Central and South America. When visiting the United Nations in New York City, she always wore traditional Quiché clothing, as a reminder of the people she was fighting to save. She was awarded the Nobel Peace Prize in 1992.

Menchú's humanitarian work is widely praised, although some people criticize the way in which she first stepped into the international spotlight. In 1983 she published *I, Rigoberta Menchú*, an account of her childhood, Mayan culture, and her family's struggle against the military. Highly acclaimed, the book was translated into 12 languages. Later, though, an anthropologist named David Stoll learned from Menchú's friends and family that a number of the autobiographical details in the book were untrue. The news, released in late 1998, shocked many. Menchú explained that she had changed some details to protect people and that she had tried to present

> "My work was mainly preparing new *compañeros* to take over the tasks that I or any of the other leaders do. In practice, the *compañeros* have to learn Spanish as I did, have to learn to read and write as I did, and assume all the responsibility for their work as I did. . . . Our experience in Guatemala has always been to be told: 'Ah, poor Indians, they can't speak.'"
>
> RIGOBERTA MENCHÚ
> *I, Rigoberta Menchú*

the plight of all her people, not just her own life. Even her critics admit that she provides an accurate idea of the situation in Guatemala. The Nobel organization hastened to assure the news media that Menchú's peace prize was in no danger of being revoked, because the positive effects of her humanitarian efforts were beyond question.

Louise Michel (1830–1905)
Anarchist, revolutionary

LOUISE MICHEL GREW UP IN VRONCOURT, FRANCE, and was educated by her grandfather, a veteran of the French Revolution. In 1856 she moved to Paris, where she taught school, wrote, and became involved with political and women's rights groups.

Michel served as a volunteer in the ambulance brigade during the Franco-Prussian War, which ended with the defeat of France in 1871. When the French National Assembly negotiated a peace treaty with the Germans that seemed to reestablish a monarchy, Republicans like Michel revolted. They formed their own government, the Paris Commune, but it was violently suppressed after just two months. Michel was imprisoned on the South Pacific island of New Caledonia. During her ten years there, she set up a school, became interested in local affairs, and continued to write.

Once freed, Michel resumed her cause, and was imprisoned several more times. She dedicated the last years of her life to public speaking. After she died in Marseilles, her body was taken to Paris and given the funeral of a national heroine.

Maria Montessori (1870–1952)
Educator, physician

MARIA MONTESSORI WAS THE FIRST WOMAN IN Italy to become a doctor, graduating from the University of Rome in 1894. This alone would have guaranteed her a place in history. But she also revolutionized early childhood education.

Starting out as a practicing surgeon, Montessori devoted more and more time to education. She began working with mentally disabled children. Her methods were so successful that some students improved enough to do regular schoolwork. In the years that followed, Montessori pursued many interests: medicine, psychology, anthropology, philosophy, and education. She spent a year as director of the Orthophrenic School, a teacher-training institute that used her techniques. Then, in 1907, she decided to apply her methods to children without disabilities. She opened the Casa dei Bambini, a day-care center for preschoolers from one of Rome's slums. By 1923 her ideas were so well respected, in America as well as Europe, that she decided to dedicate her career to promoting the "Montessori method."

Montessori's techniques reversed the traditional educational approach, in which the teacher talked while a group of students listened. Instead she focused on the child and kept teachers in the background to provide guidance. Classroom furniture was child-sized, to give students the feeling that the room was their place. She created materials that inspired students to work with them, learning along the way. Today there are Montessori schools worldwide, and even non-Montessori preschools and day-care centers often use her ideas.

Lucretia Coffin Mott (1793–1880)
Social reformer, Quaker minister, educator

OF THE MANY REFORMERS IN 19TH-CENTURY America, few were active in as wide a range of reforms as Lucretia Mott. She supported abolition, women's rights, Native American rights, religious freedom, temperance, and pacifism. Supporters of her various causes didn't always agree with each other, especially abolitionists and feminists. Mott often managed to help them work together, though. Her opposition to prejudice of any kind was contagious.

Raised a Quaker, Mott taught at a Society of Friends school before her marriage. She became a Quaker minister at the age of 28. Her powerful sermons against slavery angered the pro-slavery wing of the Quakers, but all efforts to prevent her from speaking her mind failed. In 1833 Mott participated in the founding of the American Anti-Slavery Society. She also organized women's abolitionist groups.

Mott was supposed to be a delegate at London's 1840 World Anti-Slavery Convention, along with Elizabeth Cady Stanton, but women were forbidden to participate. Outraged that men who were progressive when it came to slavery could be so backward about women's rights, Mott and Stanton agreed to work together to change that. Accordingly, they organized the 1848 women's rights convention in Seneca Falls, New York. This early meeting played an immeasurably important role in America's women's rights movement.

Mott also maintained her commitment to her religion and to education. She was one of the founders of Swarthmore, a coeducational college established by the Quakers in 1864. Near the end of her long career, she became increasingly involved with the peace movement and was active in Pennsylvania's Peace Society.

Anna Pauline (Pauli) Murray (1910–1985)
Civil rights activist, lawyer, feminist, poet, Episcopal minister

PAULI MURRAY NEVER LET OBSTACLES GET IN the way of her ambitions. Determined to go to college, she left segregated South Carolina to go to Columbia University, but the school didn't accept women. Instead she earned her degree at Hunter College. While in New York City, she socialized with the Harlem Renaissance literary crowd and began to write poetry, an activity she continued for the rest of her life.

In 1938 Murray was denied admission to the University of North Carolina because of her race. She went to Howard University, but she made sure that her illegal rejection by UNC made national news. She also joined the NAACP, becoming a high-profile civil rights leader.

Again seeking to further her training, Murray was rejected by Harvard Law School in 1944 because she was female, so she went to the University of California at Berkeley. Afterward she wrote *States' Laws on Race and Color* (1951), a highly praised work of legal scholarship, and *Proud Shoes* (1956), a biography of her grandparents. She worked at a prestigious New York law firm and taught in Ghana.

Murray became the first African American to receive a doctorate in law from Yale in 1965, and the next year, she helped to found the National Organization for Women. In 1977 she became the first black woman ordained as an Episcopal minister. She died in 1985, having achieved excellence in an astonishing variety of endeavors.

Sarojini Chattopadhyay Naidu (1879–1949)
Suffragist, activist, stateswoman, poet

AFTER GRADUATING FROM COLLEGE IN ENGLAND, Sarojini Chattopadhyay returned home to India and married Govindarajulu Naidu. This was a risk. Sarojini was a member of the highest caste of Hindus, the Brahman, or "priestly," caste, and her husband belonged to the Ksatriya, or "warrior," caste, who were considered inferior. But in this, as in everything, Naidu was guided by her own convictions above all.

Naidu had participated in the women's suffrage campaign while she was in England, and she became an activist in India, too. Fighting to improve women's status, she condemned *purdah*, the custom of secluding women that was practiced by both Hindus and Muslims. She also worked with Mahatma Gandhi in his nonviolent movement to liberate India from England. In 1925 she became the first Indian woman president of the Indian National Congress. Naidu was jailed several times for her anti-British activities, but this didn't stop her. After India was granted independence in 1947, she served as governor of Uttar Pradesh until her death.

Naidu was also a respected poet. She was elected to the

Royal Society of Literature in 1914, and she presided over a famous literary salon in Bombay. In honor of her literary talent, Naidu is often called the "Nightingale of India."

Nakayama Miki (1798–1887)
Religious leader

In 1838 Nakayama Miki, the wife of a landowner in Shoyashiki, Japan, took her son to the village healer to be treated for an illness. Normally the healer worked by putting an assistant into a trance as part of the healing ritual. That day the assistant was not there, so Nakayama took her place and fell into a trance that lasted several days. She began to speak for a being she called the "Heavenly Shogun," proclaiming that, as his medium, she was released from womanly duties. Afterward, Nakayama discovered that she had healing powers. She wrote songs and poems that became the scriptures for a religion, Tenrikyo. Her followers came to regard her as a living god.

Tenrikyo emphasizes communal labor, charity, and service. It incorporates ancient Shinto concepts such as shamanistic healing and ancestor worship. In fact, it is officially a sect of the Shinto religion. Today there are over two million believers, and people from all over the world make pilgrimages to Shoyashiki, renamed Tenri City.

Carry Amelia Moore Gloyd Nation (1846–1911)
Temperance reformer

Carry Nation had an especially difficult childhood, and her brief first marriage ended when her alcoholic husband died, leaving her to raise a child alone. She often turned to religion for comfort from her troubles. In 1877 she remarried and moved with her husband to Texas, where a religious experience convinced her that she was chosen by God to fight evil. From then on, Nation became a crusader against alcohol.

After settling in Kansas, Nation helped establish a local chapter of the Woman's Christian Temperance

Union in 1892. The State had outlawed the sale of liquor in 1880, but saloons continued to operate. Somehow the owners never got into trouble for breaking the law. Nation and other temperance supporters tried to stop them in the usual ways—with prayer, song, and talk. They closed a few bars, but progress was slow. Then in 1900, Nation took a different approach.

Carrying a hatchet and loudly singing a hymn, she burst into a saloon, smashing the bar and everything in it. For a short while, these destructive tactics were effective. The dramatic, emotional approach appealed to a lot of people. Nation performed "hatchetations" on several saloons around Kansas. She was often arrested and accumulated so many fines that she had to go on the lecture circuit and even sold tiny souvenir hatchets to raise money.

By 1904, though, Nation's fame was fading. Her increasingly poor health made travel difficult, and she lectured less and less often. She died in obscurity in 1911, nearly a decade before Prohibition began.

Agnes Nestor (1880–1948)
Labor activist

Agnes Nestor moved to Chicago and started work at the Eisendrath Glove Company in 1897. She found her coworkers already at the brink of rebellion. They sewed gloves for at least 12 hours a day, the wages were low, the rooms were hot and cramped—and to top it all off they had to pay rent for the machines and buy their own needles! By spring of 1898, the women went on strike. In just ten days, with Nestor as their spokesperson, they succeeded in ending the "machine rent" and unionizing the shop.

Nestor was a natural labor leader, having been schooled by her Irish-born father in the methods of trade unionism. By 1906 she was given a paid position in the National Glove Workers Union and served the organization for the rest of her life.

A promoter of all working women's rights, she was active in the Chicago and National Women's Trade Union Leagues. Her lobbying skills secured Illinois's Ten-Hour-Day Law in 1909. But she continued to fight for what she really wanted, an eight-hour maximum day. That law finally passed in 1937.

Florence Nightingale (1820–1910)
Health care reformer

BORN INTO A WELL-TO-DO ENGLISH FAMILY, Florence Nightingale upset her genteel parents when she said she wanted to be a nurse. In the 1840s, hospitals were filthy places, and nurses were untrained women with a bad moral reputation. But Nightingale persisted and finally persuaded her father to let her train in Germany. By 1853 she was well respected as the superintendent of the Institution for the Care of Sick Gentlewomen in London.

In 1854 the British were engaged in a bloody war against Russia on the Crimean Peninsula. Nightingale led a group of volunteer nurses to the army hospital there. The doctors, embarrassed at needing help, ignored the women at first. But there were soon too many wounded to refuse aid.

> "No *man*, not even a doctor, ever gives any other definition of what a nurse should be than this—'devoted and obedient.' This definition would do just as well for a porter. It might even do for a horse. It would not do for a policeman."
>
> FLORENCE NIGHTINGALE
> *Notes on Nursing*, 1860

Nightingale distinguished herself there in every way. She introduced life-saving sanitary practices. She was willing to work at even the lowliest jobs and was called the "Lady with the Lamp," because she tended so many patients in the middle of the night.

Welcomed as a national hero when she returned home in 1856, Nightingale refused all public celebration of her work. She was exhausted from the war and took to her bed, directing others to carry out her far-reaching reforms. She pushed the army to change its medical practices and, in 1860, established the landmark Nightingale School for Nurses. In 1907 she became the first woman to be awarded the Order of Merit by the king.

Mildred Norman ("Peace Pilgrim") (1908–1981)
Pacifist

MILDRED NORMAN'S OLDEST FRIENDS REMEMBER her as intelligent, active, and even a little vain—she wore makeup and liked clothes. There was no hint that in the future she would become a modern-day pilgrim, traveling by foot and encouraging everyone she met to seek inner peace and work for world harmony.

Her spiritual awakening came suddenly, at age 30, when she spent a night walking in the woods, pondering her life and unhappy marriage. Soon she separated from her husband and concentrated on her spiritual quest.

She began her pilgrimage in 1953, walking all the way from California to the East Coast. There, she delivered petitions calling for peace in Korea, worldwide disarmament, and the creation of a United States

Peace Department. Then she turned around and kept walking. She crossed the country six times before her accidental death in 1981.

Peace Pilgrim carried her few belongings in the pockets of her blue shirt. She accepted food and shelter only when they were offered and otherwise did without. Although she endured taunts and vagrancy arrests, most of the people who met her or heard her speak felt they had been changed for the better. Her work is kept alive by the California group, Friends of the Peace Pilgrim.

Caroline Sheridan Norton (1808–1877)
Activist for married women's rights, writer

CAROLINE SHERIDAN'S MARRIAGE TO GEORGE Norton was difficult from the start. George was unreasonable, even violent, and chronically short of money. Caroline supported the family herself, writing novels, plays, poems, and essays. When she obtained a legal separation in 1836, her husband sued her, falsely claiming she had had an affair with the prime minister, Lord Melbourne. Although the adultery charge was dismissed, Caroline's reputation was harmed. Even worse, George refused to let her see her children. Her fierce fight for custody rights

led to the Infant Custody Bill of 1839, granting mothers certain minimum contacts with their children. Personally, however, Caroline's campaign was less successful. Her youngest child died before she managed to arrange visitation rights.

In 1855 Caroline again found herself in a struggle with George Norton, when he demanded a share of the money she earned from her successful writing career. Outraged, she wrote to Queen Victoria. This time her efforts helped to speed the passage of the Marriage and Divorce Act of 1857, bolstering the rights of married women.

George Norton died in 1875, and Caroline was free to remarry. Sadly, she died a few months after marrying her longtime friend, Sir William Stirling-Maxwell.

Emmeline Pankhurst (1858–1928)
Christabel Pankhurst (1880–1958)
Sylvia Pankhurst (1882–1960)
Adela Pankhurst (1885–1961)
Suffragists

THE PANKHURSTS, AN ENTIRE FAMILY OF SUFFRAGIST activists, played a leading role in England's voting rights movement. Emmeline and her husband, the attorney Richard Pankhurst, focused on suffrage and property rights issues through legislative means during the late 1800s. When her husband died in 1898, Emmeline withdrew from public life until her daughter Christabel inspired her to return to activism, this time taking a more militant stance. In 1903 Emmeline and Christabel formed the Women's Social and Political Union. Christabel's sisters, Sylvia and Adela, supported the group at first, but by 1911 had both embarked on different paths.

At first the WSPU slogan, "deeds not words," meant graffitied buildings, protest marches, and disrupted government meetings. But years passed, and the British government continued to ignore their demands. So the WSPU decided to increase the pressure. By 1908 members regularly smashed windows and set unoccupied buildings on fire.

All the violent actions by the WSPU were met with arrests, but the suffragists did not let that put an end to their protests. Imprisoned, they refused to eat or drink. The British government responded with the "Cat and Mouse" Act of 1913, in which the police were the cats and the inmates were mice. Women who made themselves sick from fasting were released. But as soon as they recovered, the police put them back in jail. Emmeline was jailed 12 times in one year under this system.

After World War I began in 1914, Christabel and Emmeline decided to put the war effort ahead of suffrage. Their demonstration of competence and patriotism did much to advance the women's rights cause among British politicians. Sylvia, who opposed World War I, joined the Women's International League for Peace and Freedom. After the war she continued to work for women's rights and socialism, later becoming active in the Ethiopian independence movement. Adela, who had moved to Australia after a disagreement with Emmeline, was a pacifist during the war and eventually became a nurse for mentally retarded children. After 1920 Christabel became a Christian evangelist. England approved universal suffrage in 1928, just weeks before Emmeline Pankhurst's death.

Maud Wood Park (1871–1955)
Suffragist

AS A STUDENT AT RADCLIFFE COLLEGE IN 1900, Maud Wood Park was disturbed to find that few of her classmates cared about women's rights. After all, they wouldn't even have been allowed to go to college if early feminists like Lucy Stone hadn't paved the way. The next year she cofounded the College Equal Suffrage League and toured the nation, inspiring 30 schools to open chapters. Park went on to become a respected political lobbyist. She had a strong grasp of legal issues, a dignified manner, and a reputation for discretion. In 1916 Carrie Chapman Catt handpicked her to lead NAWSA's congressional committee in the final suffrage battles, assuring the passage of the 19th Amendment.

After women's right to vote was secure, Park served as the first president of the National League of Women Voters, focusing the group on a wide variety of issues, including education and economic reform. Thanks to the lobbying efforts of another of her endeavors, the Women's Joint Congressional Committee, key pieces of legislation protecting children and immigrant women were passed.

Retiring to Maine after 1928, Park took up writing, the career she would have chosen if reform work had not chosen her. She wrote over 20 plays, including *Lucy Stone*, a tribute to one of her earliest role models.

Rosa Parks (1913–)
Civil rights activist

ROSA PARKS'S STORY SHOWS HOW ONE QUIET action can ripple into rings of change. On December 1, 1955, Parks took the bus home from work as usual. At that time in Alabama, buses were segregated: White people sat in front, while black people sat in back and were expected to stand if the bus was crowded. That evening, the white section filled, and the driver told Parks to give up her seat. She refused and was arrested.

Seven thousand African Americans met to protest Parks's arrest. They formed the Montgomery Improvement Association and made the young Reverend Martin Luther King, Jr. its president.

At her trial Parks was found guilty and ordered to pay a fine. Outraged, the black community swore to boycott buses for as long as it took to get justice. They walked, took taxis, or drove—no matter what, they did not set foot on a bus. The boycott lasted

more than a year, but it was a success. Meanwhile, Parks's case went all the way to the Supreme Court, which ruled that the buses must be integrated. Dr. King emerged as a national leader. The peaceful methods of boycotts and sit-ins spread throughout the South.

Parks and her husband, however, lost their jobs as a result of her stand. Moving to Detroit, Parks worked for Michigan Representative John Conyers and remained politically active. In 1992 she published her autobiography, *My Story*.

Alice Paul (1885–1977)
Suffragist, social reformer

ALICE PAUL WAS ORIGINALLY A MEMBER OF THE National American Woman Suffrage Association, but she thought their legislative strategy in the fight for suffrage was too quiet and too slow. A native of New Jersey, Paul had spent time at graduate school in England, where she had participated in the Pankhursts' militant women's suffrage campaign. Inspired by that experience, she left NAWSA in 1913 to form the Congressional Union for Woman Suffrage— later renamed the National Woman's party.

Paul's provocative and highly visible tactics varied. She planned protest marches and hunger strikes, as well as publicity campaigns. On the eve of Woodrow Wilson's inauguration as president in 1913, she organized 5,000 women for a peaceful march to the White House, a demonstration that sparked a riot. Some protests led by Paul were sedate: a parade of cars unfurling a suffrage petition over three miles (5 km) long, and pro-vote valentines mailed to members of Congress. Others were violent. NWP protesters suffered police brutality and were frequently arrested. Paul herself was force-fed, involuntarily committed to a psychiatric ward, and put in solitary confinement.

After the passage of the 19th Amendment, Paul became a lawyer and began to promote women's rights at the international level. She wrote the first draft of the Equal Rights Amendment to the United States Constitution in 1923 and spent the rest of her life campaigning for it. The Amendment, sometimes called the "Alice Paul Amendment," remains a dream unrealized.

Elizabeth Palmer Peabody (1804–1894)
Educator, publisher, transcendentalist

BORN INTO AN INTELLECTUAL MASSACHUSETTS family, Elizabeth Peabody was educated at the Franklin Academy, where her mother was headmistress. She entered the field of education as well, becoming a teacher and opening her own schools. In 1834 she helped Bronson Alcott establish his famous Temple School in Boston.

Peabody was one of the most influential followers of transcendentalism, a religious philosophy native to mid-19th century New England. The transcendentalists, who included Alcott, Ralph Waldo Emerson, and Margaret Fuller, believed that people were fundamentally good and that spiritual enlightenment could be achieved through contemplation, without formal religious structure. Peabody was the proprietor of the West Street bookstore, the group's unofficial headquarters. She also operated a press, publishing works by Fuller, Nathaniel Hawthorne, and others.

True to her upbringing, Peabody believed that the key to the success of transcendentalism was in early education. Inspired by the German educator Friedrich Froebel, Peabody applied her philosophy to his concept of the kindergarten. She opened her first kindergarten in 1860 and founded the American Froebel Union in 1877. A teacher and writer until the end of her life, Peabody continued to promote kindergartens and related educational reforms, including schooling for African Americans and Native Americans.

Anne-Madeleine Pelletier (1874–1939)
Feminist, pacifist, journalist

DURING HER CAREER, MADELEINE PELLETIER associated with Socialists, Communists, and Anarchists, but none of those groups were committed enough to her causes. In the end, she worked alone. Pelletier, who carried a cane and wore a bowler hat and a tie, became the first female doctor hired at Paris's Assistance Publique in 1899.

Pelletier believed that war distracted workers from the misery inflicted on them by capitalists and kept mothers busy producing sons. An ardent suffragist, she argued that if women were allowed to vote, peace would come about naturally, because society didn't condition them to fight. Pelletier founded and edited a journal, *La suffragiste,* to advance her views. In spite of her pacifism, however, she used the violent tactics employed by England's Pankhurst family to draw attention to her feminist demands.

After 1925 Pelletier concentrated on providing health care to poor women. Whenever necessary, she advocated birth control and performed abortions, openly defying the law. Already in poor health, she was imprisoned in an asylum in 1939 and died there within the year.

Sally J. Priesand (1946–)
Rabbi

IN 1972 SALLY PRIESAND BECAME THE FIRST female to be ordained as a Reform rabbi in the United States. Other women had performed rabbinical duties from time to time, but their status was unofficial. Priesand ushered in a whole new era.

Raised in Cleveland, Ohio, by Reform Jewish parents who treated their male and female children equally, Priesand decided on her life path when she was only 16 years old. She graduated from the University of Cincinnati in 1968 with an English degree and went on to earn her master's degree in Hebrew literature from Hebrew Union College-Jewish Institute of Religion. Her first job—assistant rabbi at the Stephen Wise Free Synagogue in New

> "That Hebrew women were the most exalted of ancient women, however, does not excuse the secondary position assigned to them. The biblical concept of womanhood influenced generations to come and is in large measure responsible for the inequality that still exists today. . .The legal views expressed in the Bible reflect a society much different from our own, and they must be reinterpreted in every generation to maintain their relevance."
>
> SALLY PRIESAND
> *Judaism and the New Woman*

York City—went well. She published *Judaism and the New Woman* (1975) while she was there and later traveled across the nation on speaking tours. In 1981 Priesand became the rabbi at the Monmouth Reform Temple in Tinton Falls, New Jersey, a position she still holds.

Charlotte E. Ray (1850–1911)
Lawyer, educator

CHARLOTTE RAY WAS THE FIRST BLACK FEMALE lawyer to practice law in the United States. But, in the end, the prejudice of others forced her to close her practice.

Ray was born in New York City. Her father, the Reverend Charles Bennett Ray, was an important link in the Underground Railroad and a well-known abolitionist. As a child, Ray attended the Institution for the Education of Colored Youth in Washington, D.C., where she did well. At age 19, she took a teaching job at Howard University and dedicated her evenings to studying law. She graduated in 1872 and became the first woman admitted to the bar in Washington, D.C.

After closing her office for lack of business, she devoted herself to women's suffrage and civil rights issues. She attended the National Women's Suffrage Association Annual Convention in 1876 and joined the National Association of Colored Women in 1895. From 1879 until her retirement in 1897, she taught at public schools in Brooklyn, New York.

Ernestine Rose (1810–1892)
Women's rights activist

AFTER ERNESTINE POTOWSKI'S MOTHER DIED IN 1826, her father—the rabbi in their Polish town—arranged a marriage for her and withheld her inheritance for her husband. Although this was the Jewish custom, the strong-minded 16-year-old refused to accept it. She took her father to court and won. Leaving Poland, Ernestine traveled in Europe, then married an English silversmith named William Ella Rose. The couple immigrated to America in 1836.

They settled in New York City, where Rose found that it was illegal for married women to own property in America. She drew up a petition to change the law, but after months of effort she had gathered only five signatures. By 1840, however, Rose had enlisted the support of Elizabeth Cady Stanton and Paulina Wright Davis, and her cause gained momentum. New York became the first state to grant married women property rights in 1848.

Rose was involved in many social reforms, including abolition, temperance, and civil rights. She was especially active in the National Woman Suffrage Association. She returned to England in the late 1860s to recuperate from an illness and spent the remaining decades of her life there.

Alice Salomon (1872–1948)
Feminist, social worker

ALICE SALOMON, FOUNDER OF THE FIRST SOCIAL work school in Germany, was born to a Jewish family in Berlin. She studied at the University of Berlin, and became one of the first German women to earn a Ph.D. in 1906. Her doctoral dissertation was about the unequal pay earned by women in the workplace.

Convinced early on of the importance of helping the needy, she was only 21 years old when she established yearlong training programs for women interested in social welfare. Eventually the courses were extended to two years and conducted under the name *Soziale Frauenschule* (Social Women's School). Salomon was active in the institution until 1933, when the new Nazi government forced her to leave her job.

Salomon was also an internationally renowned feminist. She had been a founder of the International Congress of Women in 1904, and she remained active in the group for years, serving as vice-president in 1920. After settling in New York City in 1937, she lectured about social work. The school she founded, which was named after her in 1932, is still operating in Berlin.

Margaret Sanger (1879–1966)
Birth control activist

MARGARET SANGER, PIONEER AND LEADER OF America's birth control movement, had seen her mother's health weakened by 18 pregnancies. She had worked as a nurse among the poor women living on New York City's Lower East Side who struggled to feed their ever-growing families. Sanger felt that if women were freed from the dangers and demands of constant childbearing, they would be on their way to liberation.

In 1912 Sanger began the risky business of publishing information about birth control. It was illegal even for doctors to tell their patients how to prevent a pregnancy. Nevertheless, she started a magazine called *Woman Rebel* and wrote a how-to pamphlet called *Family Limitation*, which she distributed secretly. Somehow she avoided arrest.

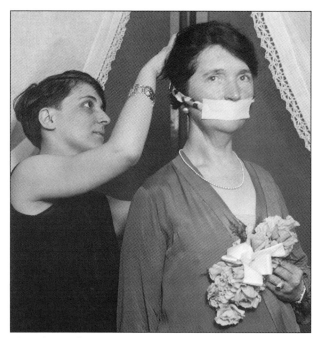

An assistant ties a gag on Margaret Sanger as part of a protest against censorship.

Sanger opened the first birth control clinic in America in 1916. It operated for just ten days before the police closed it down. Her arrest and trial gained national attention. On appeal, the court ruled that doctors should be allowed to advise women about birth control under certain circumstances. Still, Sanger had to stock her clinics through clandestine methods. She imported diaphragms from Germany in containers disguised as oil drums.

Sanger's dedication to her cause paid off, step by step. In 1921 she founded the American Birth Control League, which is active today as the Planned Parenthood Federation of America. In 1937 the American Medical Association recommended educating medical students about how to prevent pregnancy. After World War II, public concern about population growth gave added support to Sanger's arguments. Even the birth control pill was introduced during her lifetime—in 1960—fulfilling Sanger's dream of a female-controlled, non-barrier method of family planning.

Phyllis Stewart Schlafly (1924–)
Political activist, anti-feminist, writer

PHYLLIS SCHLAFLY HAS DEDICATED HER CAREER to promoting conservative political issues and has made a particular point of opposing feminism. She argues that powerful, intelligent women—like herself—should recognize their differences from men and use their skills accordingly.

Schlafly entered Republican politics in 1945, immediately after receiving her master's in political

science from Radcliffe College. In 1964 she became the vice-president of the National Federation of Republican Women and started the Eagles Trust Fund to support conservative political candidates.

In 1972 she began her campaign against the Equal Rights Amendment. She felt that the amendment, which required men and women to be treated equally under the law, would cause women to abandon their responsibilities to home and family. She spoke out against the ERA on radio and on television, testified against it in front of 30 state legislatures, and published a book, *The Power of a Positive Woman*, in 1977. Her lobbying groups, Stop ERA and the Eagle Forum, backed up her efforts. The ERA was defeated in 1982. Schlafly continues to support Republican causes.

Sophie Scholl (1921–1943)
Resistance fighter

WHEN HITLER CAME TO POWER IN 1933, Sophie Scholl and her brothers and sisters were as inspired as most Germans by his patriotic speeches about the "Fatherland." The Scholl boys joined the Hitler Youth, and the girls joined the League of German Girls. But it always bothered Sophie that her Jewish friends were excluded.

Gradually Sophie learned of the repressiveness of the Nazi regime, and by the time war was declared in 1939, she was fiercely opposed to Hitler. Entering the University of Munich in 1942, she joined the White Rose, a war resistance group cofounded by her older brother Hans. The group secretly produced leaflets urging peaceful resistance to Hitler's plan. It was terribly dangerous work. They packed suitcases full of leaflets and traveled by train to distant towns. They mailed thousands of them to addresses copied from the phone book. They spray-painted anti-Nazi graffiti on walls.

On February 18, 1943, a janitor at the university caught Sophie and her brother throwing leaflets from a tower into the courtyard below. They held their tongues under interrogation, but the Gestapo found the remaining members of the group, and the White Rose was crushed. Sophie and Hans were tried on February 22nd and executed that same day.

Rosika Schwimmer (1877–1948)
Pacifist, feminist

IN 1928 HUNGARIAN-BORN ROSIKA SCHWIMMER WAS denied United States citizenship. It was a time when America was gripped with a fear of foreigners, especially those from countries associated with Germany, the enemy in World War I. However, the judges who ruled against Schwimmer were criticized—she was a world-famous pacifist. She had promoted the idea of "continuous mediation" by neutral countries to end the war and cofounded the Woman's Peace party with Jane Addams and Carrie Chapman Catt.

Through her activism and her articles for Hungarian and German papers, Schwimmer had forged an international reputation as a feminist, too. A prolific writer, she edited the journal *A Nö* (The woman), translated Charlotte Perkins Gilman's *Women and Economics* into Hungarian, and published a novel and several stories.

During the 1930s she campaigned in favor of a world government. At the time of her death, she was a nominee for the 1948 Nobel Peace Prize. It was not awarded that year because "no suitable living candidate" could be found.

Elizabeth Bayley Seton (1774–1821)
Religious leader

A NATIVE OF NEW YORK CITY, ELIZABETH BAYLEY Seton was always committed to helping the poor. While raising her five children, she devoted herself to charitable work and founded a widow's relief society in 1797. She traveled to Italy with her ailing husband in 1803, hoping in vain that the change of climate would cure him. After his death, Seton continued to take such comfort in the Roman Catholicism she had encountered in Europe that she converted in 1805. Her family and friends—devout Episcopals—were upset by her decision; many refused to associate with her.

In 1808 Seton moved to Maryland, where there was a larger Catholic community, and opened a girls' school at St. Mary's College in Baltimore. Her religious dedication continued to grow. The next year, Seton took vows and helped to form the first American-based Catholic sisterhood, later known as the Sisters of Charity of St. Joseph. Moving their religious community to Emmitsburg, Maryland, the sisters opened a school, and Mother Seton invited poor girls in the area to attend. Steadily, the sisterhood grew from 16 women to a national network. In 1975 Mother Seton's dedication was honored when she became the first American-born woman to be canonized as a saint.

Betty Shabazz (1936–1997)
Civil rights leader, educator

WHEN CIVIL RIGHTS LEADER MALCOLM X WAS assassinated on February 21, 1965, his wife, Betty Shabazz, pregnant with twins, threw herself in front of their four children to protect them from the flying bullets. Throughout her life, Shabazz continued this role as protector of her family and her people. She dedicated herself to keeping her husband's legacy alive, emphasizing that, before his death, Malcolm turned away from the militant tactics he had advocated as leader of the Nation of Islam.

After the assassination, Shabazz, a registered nurse, went on with her work in public health. She earned a doctorate in education in 1975, eventually becoming an administrator at Medgar Evers College in Brooklyn, New York. She spoke about black history, race relations, and civil rights at ceremonies in honor of Malcolm X, and remained an active public presence.

Shabazz believed that Louis Farrakhan, who succeeded Malcolm as head of the Nation of Islam, was responsible for the assassination. This may have led indirectly to her own tragic death. In 1995 Shabazz's daughter Qubilah tried to hire a friend to kill Farrakhan and, as a result, was ordered by the court to undergo psychiatric and drug treatment. While she

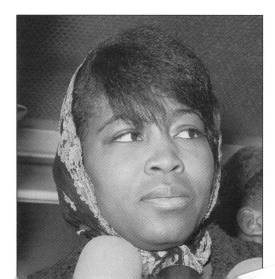

completed the program, her 12-year-old son lived with Shabazz. The boy, in an incomprehensible act, set fire to the house on June 1, 1997, and Shabazz sustained fatal burns.

Eleanor Smeal (1939–)
Feminist, political scientist

ELEANOR SMEAL JOINED THE NATIONAL Organization for Women when it first formed in 1970, and her advancement in the group was swift. By the next year, she was president of the local chapter in South Hills, Pennsylvania. The year after that, she became head of the Pennsylvania state NOW. She was elected to the first of her three terms as NOW's national president in 1977. With characteristic efficiency and determination, she cleared the group's debt, doubled membership, and organized two major marches in Washington, D.C. The first, which was held in 1979, demanded the passage of the Equal Rights Amendment. The second took place in 1986, during the conservative Reagan era, and centered on abortion rights.

Educated as a political scientist, Smeal was the first to pinpoint the "gender gap"—the fact that men and women tend to vote differently. She wrote about this in her book, *Why and How Women Will Elect the Next President* (1984).

Smeal now leads the Feminist Majority, which she founded in 1987. In addition to lobbying for legislative change, the group provides the public with up-to-date information about issues of concern to feminists.

Elizabeth Cady Stanton (1815–1902)
Suffragist

AS A CHILD, ELIZABETH CADY STANTON WAS DEEPLY affected when her beloved father repeatedly said that he wished she were a boy. So she resolved to become as self-reliant as a man. When she married the abolitionist Henry B. Stanton in 1840, the word "obey" was left out of the marriage vows.

Stanton helped Lucretia Mott organize the first American women's rights convention, which was held in Seneca Falls, New York, in 1848. In her

Elizabeth Cady Stanton with her daughter, Harriot

speech at the convention, she called for a woman's right to get an education, enter a profession, control her own money, own property, and most shocking of all, to vote. The convention drew over 300 people, but newspapers ridiculed the event and failed to recognize its true significance.

In 1852 Stanton began to work with Susan B. Anthony. By this time, Stanton was the busy mother of seven children, and she wasn't able to travel much, so she wrote the eloquent speeches that Anthony delivered. She later described their successful collaborative relationship, saying, "I forged the thunderbolts and she fired them." Stanton and Anthony worked together to form and lead both the National Woman Suffrage Association and its later incarnation, the National American Woman Suffrage Association.

In the last decades of her life, Stanton wrote, traveled, and lectured to large audiences, becoming increasingly outspoken in favor of radical causes. Her *Woman's Bible* (1895) criticized organized religion's view of women and was condemned by many of her fellow suffragists. No matter how outrageous others found her ideas, Stanton spoke her mind. Much of the success of the early suffragist movement can be attributed to her spirited leadership.

Mabel Keaton Staupers
(1890–1989)
Nurse, civil rights activist, organization executive

As WORLD WAR II RAGED ON, MABEL KEATON Staupers tried without success to persuade the American military to increase its quotas for black nurses. In January 1945 she learned that the Army was actually considering *drafting* nurses in order to fill spots reserved for white nurses. With perfect timing, Staupers issued a public challenge: "If nurses are needed so desperately, why isn't the Army using colored nurses?" Telegrams expressing support of the cause poured into army offices. The end to quotas was declared within the month.

Staupers, who was born in Barbados, came to America when she was a girl. When she graduated from the Howard University College of Nursing in Washington, D.C., black nurses had few career opportunities. But she was determined to open doors. As executive secretary of the National Association of Colored Graduate Nurses, she cleverly used the media and political connections, even calling a meeting with Eleanor Roosevelt. Having integrated the military nurse corps was a first step, but Staupers intended to do more—to integrate the American Nurses' Association. It took another three years to get that job done. In 1951 the victorious NACGN voted itself out of existence.

Gloria Steinem (1934–)
Women's rights activist, journalist

GLORIA STEINEM WANTED TO WRITE ABOUT important issues and political events. But living in New York City in the late 1950s, she discovered it was difficult for a woman to get a job as a reporter. Steinem persevered, and by 1963 she was a full-time freelance writer for national magazines. Still, she wasn't getting the political stories she wanted. During this time, she accepted an assignment to go undercover at a nightclub as a Playboy bunny. Steinem's article exposed the sexism and discrimination at the club, but her critics refused to see beyond the fact that she had worn a revealing costume.

In 1968 Steinem helped found *New York* magazine. There she could write freely about many issues. But her

male colleagues actively discouraged her from writing about feminism, even though she was increasingly interested in the topic. So, in 1972, Steinem created *Ms.*, a magazine produced entirely by women. *Ms.* allowed Steinem and other feminists to use their talents as wordsmiths to promote their ideas. Steinem has also published several books, including *Outrageous Acts and Everyday Rebellions* (1983) and *Moving Beyond Words* (1994).

Steinem was also politically active. In 1971 she was one of the founders of the National Women's Political Caucus to help elect more women to political office, and she campaigned for the Equal Rights Amendment. The Ms. Foundation, which Steinem created, sponsors the annual "Take Our Daughters to Work Day" in April.

Lucy Stone (1818–1893)
Suffragist, abolitionist

AS A CHILD LUCY STONE PLEDGED TO LEARN GREEK and Hebrew in order to find the mistakes in the Bible's translation—she refused to believe that men were created to rule over women, as she had been taught. She also vowed never to marry, and she might have followed through with that resolution, if she hadn't met Henry Blackwell, who shared her commitment to equal rights. When they married in 1855, Stone kept her maiden name.

Stone began her public speaking career in the 1840s, braving hostile crowds to speak for the Anti-Slavery Society. The organization insisted that she talk about women's issues on her own time, though. So in 1850, she committed herself to feminism full-time and helped organize the first truly national women's rights convention in Worcester, Massachusetts. The speech she gave there inspired Susan B. Anthony as well as the philosopher John Stuart Mill.

When the suffrage movement split in two in 1869, Stone formed the American Woman Suffrage

Association and led the group for 20 years. She founded a newspaper, the *Woman's Journal*, in 1870 with her husband's help. A highly respected national publication, it continued after her death under the editorship of her daughter, Alice Blackwell.

Marie Charlotte Carmichael Stopes (1880–1958)
Birth control activist, scientist

MARIE STOPES STARTED FORMAL SCHOOLING AT THE late age of 12 and still managed to be the first woman hired to teach science at Manchester University in 1904. The following year, she became the youngest person in England to earn a Doctor of Science degree. Stopes was widely respected for her academic career as a paleobotanist, or a scientist who studies plants of prehistoric times. However, it was her work in marriage relations and family planning that brought her fame.

Not all supporters of birth control agreed on why it should be done. The most common arguments were that uncontrolled childbirth led to overpopulation and that poor parents with large families to feed just fell deeper into poverty. Stopes took a different approach. She argued that a woman's health was endangered by giving birth to so many babies. She also said that a couple could have a happier relationship if they had fewer children. In 1921, with her second husband, Humphrey V. Roe, Stopes opened England's first free birth control clinic.

The birth control movement offended many people. The Catholic Church condemned Stopes's ideas. She was so controversial that the London newspaper *The Times* refused to run a birth announcement for her child in 1924. Still, support for the movement grew. Stopes's clinic remains in operation today.

Jessie Mary Grey Street (1889–1970)
Feminist, social reformer

TRUE TO THE PIONEERING SPIRIT OF HER FAMILY members, who had helped settle Australia and fought for women's suffrage, Jessie Street was a strong leader with a variety of interests. While she was at college in Sydney, Street formed the school's first field hockey teams. And after graduation she opened a dairy farm using imported milking machines to prove that advanced technology could help improve output. Once the success of her venture was assured, she sold the farm and went to the 1911 International Council of Women in Rome. She studied social work in New York City and then returned home to establish the Social Hygiene Association, hoping to rid Sydney of its slums. In 1918 she cofounded Sydney's League of Nations Union to promote international understanding.

By the onset of World War II, Street's activities focused most strongly on peace and feminism. She was Australia's only female delegate at the United Nations founding conference in 1945, and played an instrumental role in keeping women's issues a part of the U.N. charter. During the 1960s, she was active in native aboriginal rights in Australia.

Baroness Bertha von Suttner (1843–1914)
Pacifist, writer

THE IDEA FOR ONE OF THE MOST RESPECTED honors in the world, the Nobel Peace Prize, has an unlikely sounding source. In 1876 Alfred Nobel, a Swedish industrialist who was living in Paris, needed a housekeeper and secretary. He hired a woman named Bertha Kinsky, who came from an impoverished but noble Austrian family. She didn't stay on the job long. At her previous position as governess for the Suttner family, Bertha had fallen in love with the Baron Arthur von Suttner. Arthur's family strongly disapproved of the match, so Bertha left. But after only a few weeks'

The Uses of Dynamite

The young Alfred Nobel was fascinated with the possibility of using the explosive nitroglycerine to help clear rock when building bridges, tunnels, or railroads. He experimented tirelessly with the dangerous substance, even after his brother was killed during a laboratory accident. Eventually, he devised a stable mixture of nitroglycerine and silica that could be detonated in controlled ways. He patented his discovery in 1867, calling it "dynamite." Many years later, Nobel's friend Bertha von Suttner frankly expressed her concerns about dynamite. It could so easily be turned into a weapon of mass destruction during wartime. Many people were surprised when Nobel's will revealed that money earned from explosives would be used to fund a peace prize.

separation from each other, the young couple decided to elope.

Bertha von Suttner went on to become a respected novelist and pacifist. She founded an antiwar group in 1891, and her novel, *Die Waffen nieder!* (1892, Lay down your arms!), helped to raise public awareness of peace issues. She edited an international antiwar journal named after the book from 1892 to 1899.

Suttner also remained friends with Nobel, and they corresponded regularly. After his death in 1896, Nobel's will provided for the establishment of, among other awards, a peace prize, which Suttner herself received in 1905.

Mother Teresa (1910–1997)
Roman Catholic missionary

AGNES GONXHA BOJAXHIU WAS BORN IN ALBANIA (now Macedonia). She knew by the time she was 12 years old that she wanted be a Catholic nun, and at 21, she took her vows, becoming Sister Teresa. At her own request, she was sent to Calcutta, India. There, in 1945, she experienced a "call within a call," convincing her that her divine mission was to live and work with the suffering people of the city's miserable slums.

It took two years for Sister Teresa to get Rome's permission to leave the convent. Finally in 1947, she underwent three months of medical training and set out into the streets alone. She began by starting a school in the simplest possible way: calling a small group of children together and teaching them outdoors. Her work was soon recognized; volunteer labor and donated funds made it possible for her to broaden her scope. In 1950 Sister Teresa became Mother Superior of a new order, the Missionaries of Charity.

Mother Teresa and her nuns gave food, clothes, medical care, education, and—most significantly—comfort to the poor. The mission also expanded to other countries. An American branch opened in the South Bronx area of New York City in 1971. Mother Teresa received many awards, including the 1979 Nobel Peace Prize. She always used the income to help more people. A limousine once given to her by Pope Paul VI was raffled off to fund a leper colony. Her simple mission of love and tenderness touched countless lives. She passionately defended traditional

National Association of Colored Women. She supported women's suffrage and international peace. As a professional lecturer and writer, she spoke out against lynching and Jim Crow laws, and worked to bring black achievements to public attention. Because of her light coloring—her paternal grandfather was white—she sometimes passed for white, a disguise she used only occasionally and always with resentment that it was necessary.

Terrell seemed to become more active with age. Her efforts to integrate the American Association of University Women succeeded when she was 85. Four years later, she marched at the head of picket lines to protest the segregation of restaurants in Washington, D.C.

Catholic values, speaking out against divorce, contraception, and abortion.

By the time of her death at the age of 87, Mother Teresa had opened 517 Missionaries of Charity outposts around the world. Over 4,500 nuns had joined the order, and they were aided in their work by tens of thousands of devoted lay volunteers. They continue to operate under the guidance of Mother Teresa's chosen successor, Sister Nirmala.

Sojourner Truth (1797?–1883)
Abolitionist, women's rights supporter, preacher

ISABELLA BAUMFREE WAS A SLAVE ON THE FARM OF John Dumont when the 1817 New York Emancipation Act was passed, requiring all slaves to be freed by 1828. Dumont promised Isabella that she could leave in 1827, a year early, but the time came, and he refused to let her go. So she fled to New York City. There she searched for her son, who had been taken from her when he was five. Discovering that he

Mary Eliza Church Terrell (1863–1954)
Teacher, civil rights activist

MARY TERRELL GREW UP UNDER PRIVILEGED circumstances for a black woman in Memphis, Tennessee, at the end of the 19th century. Her father, who had become a millionaire through real estate investment, sent her to Oberlin College and on a two-year tour of Europe. After an initial protest, he supported her decision to become a teacher. He had wanted her to be a "real lady" of leisure.

Marriage and motherhood ended Terrell's teaching career, but she began an active life of community service. In 1896 she was elected president of the

had been sold illegally out-of-state, Isabella sued to get the boy back and won, an unusual accomplishment for a black woman of the time.

In 1843 Isabella heard voices telling her to change her name to Sojourner Truth and become a traveling preacher. She turned out to be an exceptionally powerful speaker. Impressively tall, she captivated audiences with her unwavering gaze and her eloquent words. Becoming active in the abolitionist cause, she spoke about black suffering whenever she preached. She helped to secure supplies for volunteer soldiers and served as a nurse during the Civil War.

Truth also spoke out for women's rights. She became famous for her "Ain't I a Woman?" speech, delivered in Ohio in 1851, and went on to work for the American Equal Rights Association. Her autobiography, as dictated to Olive Gilbert—Truth never learned to write—was called *The Narrative of Sojourner Truth: A Northern Slave* (1850).

Harriet Tubman (1820?–1913)
Abolitionist

Harriet Tubman was born a slave in Dorchester County, Maryland. While still just a small child, she labored all day in the house or in the fields. When she was 13, a cruel overseer hit

"Moses" in the Reeds

Harriet Tubman's rescues were filled with hair-raising close calls. Once, at what had been a station on the Underground Railroad, a white stranger answered the door and said the house's owner had been chased away for helping blacks. Alarmed, Tubman hurried her group to a swamp outside town. They hid, miserable and damp and hungry, in the reeds. Hours passed. Finally, a Quaker strolled by. He seemed to be mumbling to himself absent-mindedly, but Tubman distinctly heard him say he had left a wagon nearby for them. It was true, and they joyfully went on their way. Tubman never discovered how the Quaker knew she needed help.

her on the head, nearly killing her. She suffered side effects from this blow for the rest of her life.

Tubman escaped from the South in 1849. Traveling alone, she followed the Underground Railroad, a network of hideouts run by abolitionists who gave runaway slaves food, supplies, and shelter. The fugitives hid in the daytime and followed the North Star by night, singing directions to one another in secret code. Once free, Tubman risked her life 19 times to rescue others, many of them family members who had been too frightened to escape with her initially. She led her missions as if they were military maneuvers, and every one of the more than 300 slaves who followed Harriet Tubman arrived safely in the North. She became known as the "Moses of her people."

During the Civil War, Tubman continued to risk her life. She served as a Union scout and spy in South Carolina, and tended wounded soldiers whenever she was needed. Although she was promised a Federal pension for her service, she never received all the money she deserved and ended her life in poverty. She was buried, however, with military honors at Fort Hill Cemetery in Auburn, New York.

Lillian D. Wald (1867–1940)
Nurse, social worker

After Vassar College rejected Lillian Wald's application, she led a rather frivolous life for several years before suddenly deciding to become a nurse in 1889. After attending the New York City Hospital Nursing School, she went on to study at the New York Infirmary. One day in 1893, she visited a patient in a tenement apartment on the Lower East Side. The poverty she encountered shocked her. Quitting school, Wald enlisted the help of her colleague Mary Brewster, and they moved into the neighborhood to provide health care. Their organization, which grew into the Henry Street Settlement, eventually expanded beyond public health nursing to include job skill training, education, and cultural and recreational programs. Wald, increasingly influential in her field, became the cofounder and president of the National Organization for Public Health Nursing in 1912.

Wald also joined other reform movements. She worked with Florence Kelley to form the Child Labor Committee in 1904. Wald, Kelley, and Jane

Addams created the American Union Against Militarism in 1914, hoping to end World War I peacefully. She detailed her career in the memoirs, *The House on Henry Street* (1915) and *Windows on Henry Street* (1934).

Faye Wattleton (1943–)
Birth control activist, feminist

AS A MATERNITY NURSE DURING THE 1960S, FAYE Wattleton witnessed the inadequacy of family planning education in America. Because abortion was illegal, many women took desperate measures to end unwanted pregnancies, leading to terrible injuries, even death. As a result, Wattleton became increasingly involved in public health and political activism. In 1977 she was elected head of the Planned Parenthood Federation of America, founded seven decades earlier by Margaret Sanger.

Wattleton was not only the first female president of the PPFA, she was also the youngest, and the first African American. She increased the group's staff and expanded its budget, all the while struggling against violent antiabortion protesters and a growing number of financial hardships imposed by Ronald Reagan's presidential administration. Her message remained consistent: All women, rich or poor, should know how to prevent unwanted pregnancy and, if that failed, they needed safe and legal abortions. She fought the federal

"gag-rule" proposed in the 1980s to prevent clinics from providing abortion information to their patients. She also worked to fund birth control research and AIDS-related programs.

Wattleton left the PPFA in 1992 but continues to work for change. Since 1995 she has been president of the Center for Gender Equity, a nonprofit institute dedicated to winning full equality for women.

Sarah Weddington (1945–)
Pro-choice activist, lawyer

IN 1970 SARAH WEDDINGTON AGREED TO HELP THE Texas women's movement to challenge a state law banning abortion. The 25-year-old lawyer had little experience, but she enlisted the help of her husband, Ron—also a lawyer—and a former classmate named Linda Coffee to plan a strategy. They took up the cause of a young waitress, Norma McCorvey, who wanted to end her pregnancy, and a married couple who were concerned that the antiabortion law violated their civil rights.

Weddington argued McCorvey's case before the Fifth Circuit Court in Texas and twice before the Federal Supreme Court. At last, in 1973, the landmark case *Roe v. Wade* was decided in her favor. With

After Jane Roe

Norma McCorvey's life did not return to normal after *Roe v. Wade*. During the trial she was known as "Jane Roe," to protect her identity, but in 1984, instead of remaining anonymous, she revealed her name and became active with the pro-choice movement. Her 1994 memoir, *I Am Roe*, described her difficult early life and her experiences during the trial. However, the next year McCorvey was befriended by members of the Christian pro-life group Operation Rescue, and she soon realized that she agreed with them. Since then she has devoted herself to trying to reverse the *Roe v. Wade* decision. Her most recent book is entitled *Won by Love* and was published in 1998.

certain exceptions, it was declared unconstitutional to bar women's access to safe and legal abortions.

During the 1970s Weddington's career took flight. She served three terms in the Texas legislature and became an adviser to President Jimmy Carter. But in the 1980s, the political climate became more conservative. Many people doubt that Weddington can ever again hold political office, because she is simply too outspoken about her pro-choice views. She continues to lecture about the constitutional right-to-privacy and teaches history and government at the university level. Her book, *A Question of Choice,* appeared in 1992.

Ida Bell Wells-Barnett (1862–1931)
Antilynching activist, teacher, journalist

I N 1884 IDA WELLS, A TEACHER IN MEMPHIS, Tennessee, refused to ride in the designated "colored" car of a train and was physically removed. Her subsequent lawsuit charging discrimination was successful at first. However, the State Supreme Court reversed the ruling on appeal three years later. Wells published an article about her experiences in court and soon began to write about other civil rights issues, too.

Fired from her teaching job in 1891 for criticizing the education black children received in segregated schools, she became editor of the *Free Speech and Headlight.* In 1892 three black men were lynched, or hanged, by a group of whites in Memphis. Wells wrote an article maintaining that they had been murdered because their businesses were competing successfully with those of their white neighbors.

After that her own life was in danger, so Wells moved to New York City. There she wrote for the *New York Age* and formed antilynching societies throughout the Northeast. Her book, *Red Record* (1895), provided a history of lynching and showed that the crime was still common.

Wells married a Chicago lawyer named Ferdinand Barnett in 1895 and went on to raise a family, but she didn't give up activist work. Among other projects, Wells-Barnett organized the Alpha Club of Chicago, America's first black women's

suffrage association; was a founder of the NAACP; worked for the National Equal Rights League; and ran, although unsuccessfully, for a seat in the Illinois State Senate.

Emma Hart Willard (1787–1870)
Educator

E MMA HART WAS AS HIGHLY EDUCATED AS A WOMAN of her time could be. She taught herself geometry at the age of 12, attended the best girls' schools in Connecticut, and became a schoolteacher. In 1807 she married John Willard and moved to Vermont. Her nephew was a student at nearby Middlebury College, and he frequently visited the Willards. Talking to him convinced Emma that even though her education had been good, men simply had access to better schools.

In 1814 Willard opened a girls' school of her own, having prepared herself to teach college-level classes. She also wrote the *Plan for Improving Female Education* (1819) and presented it to the New York state legislature. The pamphlet, which requested government financing for a school, earned praise from both Thomas Jefferson and John Adams. Governor DeWitt Clinton didn't authorize money, but he approved a school charter, so Willard moved to Waterford, New York.

In Waterford books and supplies were few, but her students prospered. When the town of Troy offered her funding in 1821, she established the Troy Female Seminary, which offered more courses in history, science, and mathematics than had ever been available to American women. While running the school, Willard wrote textbooks and poetry. Even after her retirement, she continued to campaign for public funding of women's education and other women's rights issues.

Frances Elizabeth Caroline Willard (1839–1898)
Temperance advocate, suffragist, educator

T HE TITLE OF ONE OF FRANCES WILLARD'S MANY pamphlets is "Do Everything." This accurately reflects the frontier attitude she learned as a child in the Wisconsin Territory. And it certainly applies to her career. While promoting temperance, she worked tirelessly to associate her cause with nearly every other 19th-century reform, a process she called "home protection."

Willard turned to temperance after establishing her reputation as a teacher and college administrator, and she rose to prominence rapidly. A founding member of the National Woman's Christian Temperance Union in 1874, she was the group's first secretary and its president from 1879 until her death. But the progressive Willard always had to struggle for her own power, because most temperance advocates were conservative about women's role in society. Willard created nearly 40 separate WCTU departments, each dedicated to the connection between a cause—health and hygiene, international peace, prison reform—and temperance. At the national convention in 1880, she influenced members to declare support for suffrage, although they balked the next year when she pressed for her Home Protection party to engage directly in politics.

At the end of her life, Willard was quite popular. Thousands attended memorial services held for her nationwide. But she never did convince the WCTU to adopt her broad vision. The union soon narrowed its focus to concentrate solely on prohibition.

Jody Williams (1950–)
Peace activist

JODY WILLIAMS DISCOVERED HER TALENT FOR defending people while she was still a girl growing up in Brattleboro, Vermont. She stood up for her brother Stephen, who is deaf, whenever bullies at school tried to tease him. As a young woman, Williams went on to study international relations and began a career as an activist.

During the 1980s, Williams worked in Latin America with such organizations as Medical Aid to El Salvador. While there she saw the terrible injuries suffered by victims of land mines. Every year 26,000 people are killed or maimed after stepping on the buried explosives, usually in areas where the fighting ended long ago.

In 1991 the Vietnam Veterans of America Foundation hired Williams to lead the International Campaign to Ban Landmines. The international grassroots movement she coordinated resulted in a treaty in just six years. Over 100 nations signed—the United States did not—and, once ratified, the ban

will go into effect. Communication via the Internet, as well as the support of the late Princess Diana and the Canadian foreign minister Lloyd Axworthy helped to speed the movement's progress. Williams won the 1997 Nobel Peace Prize for her work, a victory that was announced on her 47th birthday.

Victoria Claflin Woodhull (1838–1927)
Social reformer, stockbroker

COLORFUL VICTORIA WOODHULL, BORN IN OHIO, consistently challenged society's views of what was acceptable. She and her sister, Tennessee Claflin, began as performers, giving spiritualist demonstrations in which they claimed to communicate with the dead.

Victoria and Tennessee moved to New York City in 1868, and they soon met the wealthy industrialist Cornelius Vanderbilt. He agreed to back them as proprietors of a stock brokerage firm—a first for women. The business opened in 1870 and was quite successful. That same year, even though women were not yet allowed to vote, Woodhull announced her intention to run for president of the United States in 1872. Soon afterward, Woodhull and Claflin introduced the *Weekly*, a newspaper advocating women's suffrage, birth control, dress reform, communism, and "free love"—and making their controversial views explicitly public.

> "A Vanderbilt may sit in his office and manipulate stocks or declare dividends by which in a few years he amasses fifty million dollars from the industries of the country, and he is one of the remarkable men of the age. But if a poor, half-starved child should take a loaf of bread from his cupboard to appease her hunger, she should be sent to the tombs."
>
> VICTORIA WOODHULL
> **Campaign speech, 1872**

Woodhull impressed suffragist leaders with her fiery voting-rights speech before Congress in early 1871. But her ideas were too extreme, so they didn't support her candidacy. Undeterred, she formed the Equal Rights party, naming black abolitionist Frederick Douglass as her running mate, although he, too, refused to be associated with her.

Woodhull's campaign, already experiencing financial problems, was further threatened in the fall of 1872, when she accused the highly respected clergyman Henry Ward Beecher of adultery. She printed the details in a special edition of the *Weekly* on November 2, 1872, and was arrested the day before the election. Charged with obscenity and libel, Woodhull was acquitted later that year.

After the election, Woodhull established a quieter public presence. In 1883 she married John Biddulph Martin, a rich English banker, and gained acceptance in London's high society. She visited the United States often to speak, though, and made two more unsuccessful bids for the presidency, in 1884 and 1892.

Clara Zetkin (1857–1933)
Socialist, Communist, feminist

CLARA ZETKIN WAS BORN IN WIDERAU, GERMANY, and educated at the Leipzig Teachers' College for Women. She was 24 years old when she first joined the German Social Democratic party.

She became internationally known for her political views after she married Ossip Zetkin, a Russian revolutionary who had been forced into exile for his Socialist activities. The pair lived in Switzerland and Paris until his death in 1889.

Zetkin and Rosa Luxemburg were close friends. The two women led the International Women's Conference against World War I in 1915 and cofounded the radical Spartacus League. From 1892 to 1917, Zetkin edited the Socialist women's paper *Die Gleichheit* (Equality).

In 1919 Zetkin joined the Communist party of Germany, and she was elected to the Reichstag, or German parliament, the following year. She served until 1932, when the Nazi government came to power—an event she had strenuously opposed. Her final months were spent in exile in Russia, where she had been active for many years as a member of the multinational association of Communists known as the Comintern.

TIME LINE

11th century B.C.E.	Binding young girls' feet to keep them small becomes popular among the Chinese nobility. It will not be outlawed until 1911.
6th century B.C.E.	The first books of the Old Testament are recorded.
43 B.C.E.	The Roman orator Hortensia leads a group of women in protesting unfair taxation.
1st century	The books of the New Testament are written down.
622	In the Middle East, Muhammad is expelled from Mecca. He will become the founder of the Muslim religion.
1337–1453	The Hundred Years' War between England and France. In 1426 Joan of Arc begins to see visions and hear voices urging her to join the French army and fight.
1441	Portuguese explorers land at Cape Blanc, Africa, and begin to capture the black inhabitants to sell as slaves in Europe.
1492	The explorer Christopher Columbus lands on an island in the Bahamas, most probably San Salvador (also called Watlings Island). He claims this New World for the Spanish King Ferdinand.
1546	English Protestant Anne Askew is executed for preaching about her faith—a public act denied to women.
1652	Englishman George Fox founds the Society of Friends, or Quakers. At the suggestion of a follower, Margaret Fell, both men and women may be ordained as ministers.
1705	English blacksmith Thomas Newcomen invents the first effective steam engine. This technological advance will make it possible to mechanize labor-intensive tasks. But it will create a new kind of hardship for factory workers and lead to the labor agitation of the 19th century.
1775–1783	The American Revolution. The Declaration of Independence is signed in July 1776.
1787	The United States Constitution is signed; it will go into effect in 1789.
1789–1799	Revolution in France. Inspired by the revolutionaries, Olympe de Gouges writes *Declaration of the Rights of Woman* in 1791.
1792	Denmark becomes the first country to abolish slavery.
1813	British reformer Elizabeth Fry visits London's Newgate Prison. Horrified by the appalling conditions endured by the prisoners, she devotes herself to improving them.
1828	The Philadelphia Female Anti-Slavery Society is founded by Lucretia Mott.
1833	Slavery is abolished in England.
1834	Women workers at a cotton mill in Lowell, Massachusetts, organize a strike after a 15 percent wage cut is announced. In Dover, New Hampshire, 800 women walk out of their mill, too, in order to support the protest.
	The sister feminists and social reformers, Angelina and Sarah Grimké, found the National Female Anti-Slavery Society and welcome women of color as members.
1839	The American abolitionist movement splits into two factions. Some abolitionists think that women should be granted broader rights, as well. Others disagree, or think that women's rights should be of secondary importance.

1844	The Lowell Female Labor Reform Association is founded in Massachusetts by Sarah Bagley.
1846	Ernestine Rose lectures across the United States about women's rights, abolition, temperance, and other progressive issues.
	Lucy Stone calls the first National Convention for Women's Rights.
1848	The first women's rights convention is held in Seneca Falls, New York.

Harriet Tubman

1849	Harriet Tubman, a slave, escapes from the South. Soon she will return and begin leading other slaves to freedom through the Underground Railroad.
1850	Elizabeth Smith Miller devises a practical gardening costume that includes pantaloons and a tunic. Miller's cousin, Elizabeth Cady Stanton, brings the outfit to the attention of several feminists, including Amelia Jenks Bloomer.
1851	Sojourner Truth delivers her famous "Ain't I a Woman" speech at a women's convention in Akron, Ohio.
1857	Aided by Caroline Norton's work, Britain's Matrimonial Causes Act is passed. It allows women to obtain a divorce more easily and assures them stronger rights afterward.
1860	The Nightingale Nursing School, named after Florence Nightingale, is founded at St. Thomas's Hospital in London.

1861–1865	The Civil War in America. Clara Barton, founder of the American Red Cross, volunteers to care for wounded soldiers.
1865	The 13th Amendment to the Constitution of the United States is ratified. It prohibits slavery or any other denial of freedom without due process of law.
1866	The American Equal Rights Association, which seeks suffrage for women and blacks, is founded by Elizabeth Cady Stanton, Susan B. Anthony, Ernestine Rose, and Martha Coffin Pelham Wright.
	Louise Michel establishes France's first feminist organization.
1868	Britain's National Society for Women's Suffrage meets for the first time.
1869	The American Woman Suffrage Association (AWSA) is founded by Lucy Stone and her husband, Henry Brown Blackwell. The AWSA seeks to establish women's suffrage state by state.
	Susan B. Anthony and Elizabeth Cady Stanton found the National Woman Suffrage Association (NWSA). They work to change the law at the federal level.
	Myra Colby Bradwell passes the Illinois State Bar Examination, but is refused admission based on her sex. That same year in Iowa, Arabella Mansfield Babb becomes the first woman admitted to the bar.
1870	British reformer Josephine Butler founds the Ladies' National Association for Repeal to fight against England's Contagious Disease Prevention Acts.
1872	Thanks to the efforts of lawyer Belva Lockwood, the United States Congress passes a law guaranteeing women equal pay for equal work in federal jobs.

American Anthony Comstock succeeds in passing the Comstock Law, which makes it illegal to import, mail, or transport "obscene" materials. Information about contraception is considered obscene.

1873   Divorced women acquire the right to hold custody of their children in England.

1874   The National Women's Christian Temperance Union is founded in Cleveland, Ohio.

1878   Emmeline Pankhurst advocates Britain's proposed Married Women's Property Act.

Emmeline Pankhurst

1879   Mary Baker Eddy founds the Church of Christ, Scientist, in Boston.

Susette "Bright Eyes" La Flesche calls for reform that results in the allotment of reservation land with citizenship rights for individual Native Americans.

1882   Dutch reformer Aletta Jacobs opens the world's first birth control clinic in Amsterdam, the Netherlands.

1890   The AWSA and the NWSA merge to form the National American Woman Suffrage Association.

1892   Ida Bell Wells-Barnett writes a defense of three black men in Memphis, Tennessee, who were lynched by a white mob.

1893   New Zealand is the first country in the world to grant women the vote on an equal basis with men.

1896   National Association of Colored Women is created. Mary Church Terrell serves as the first president.

1897   Millicent Garrett Fawcett founds the National Union of Women's Suffrage Societies in England.

1898   Agnes Nestor leads a strike at the Eisendrath Glove Factory.

1900   International Ladies' Garment Workers Union is established.

1903   The National Women's Trade Union League is established in America by middle-class and working women.

1905   Activist Madeleine Pelletier is elected secretary of the feminist Groupe de la Solidarité des Femmes in France.

1909   The National Association for the Advancement of Colored People (NAACP) is founded.

1910   At the International Socialist Women's Organization conference in Copenhagen, March 8th is declared International Women's Day at the suggestion of German reformer Clara Zetkin.

1914–1918   World War I. Jane Addams, Emily Balch, Rosika Schwimmer, Aletta Jacobs, and others form the International Committee of Women for Permanent Peace in 1915.

1917   The Russian Revolution. Revolutionary Vera Figner is elected chairperson of the country's Amnesty Committee, the purpose of which is to aid freed political prisoners.

1919   The 18th Amendment to the United States Constitution is ratified, prohibiting the sale or consumption of alcoholic beverages.

1920	The 19th Amendment to the United States Constitution grants women's suffrage. It goes into effect on August 26th.
1923	Margaret Sanger organizes the first birth control conference in the United States.
	The National Woman's party meets in Seneca Falls, New York, to endorse the Equal Rights Amendment written by Alice Paul.
1925	Reformer Sarojini Naidu is the first woman to be elected president of the Indian National Congress.
1928	All British women over 21 years old are allowed to vote. Suffrage was granted to women older than 30 a decade before.
1929	"Black Thursday," the disastrous stock market crash of October 27th, signals the beginning of the Great Depression in the United States.
1930	Reformer and educator Mary McLeod Bethune becomes President Franklin Roosevelt's only black woman adviser.
1933	Prohibition is repealed by the 21st Amendment to the United States Constitution.

Alice Salomon

1937	Internationally renowned social reformer Alice Salomon flees her home country, Germany, because the threat of the Nazi party has become too great. Settling in New York City, she resumes her work.

1939–1945	World War II. In 1942 a group of students in Munich, Germany, found the underground anti-Nazi group, the White Rose.
1943	Rosa Parks is named secretary of her Montgomery, Alabama, chapter of the NAACP.
1946	Japanese women are given the right to vote.
1947	England withdraws from its Indian colonies, which separate into two independent countries, predominantly Hindu India and Muslim Pakistan.
1948	In South Africa, the National Party comes to power. Within a year a new policy of racial segregation, apartheid, is in place.
1950–1953	The Korean War. In an effort to prevent the expansion of communism in the area, the United States and the United Nations join the fighting on the side of the South Koreans.
1954	The Supreme Court case *Brown v. The Board of Education* establishes that racial segregation in schools is unconstitutional.

Helen Keller with her pet dog

1956	*The Miracle Worker*, a play written by William Gibson and based on the life of Helen Keller, is a great success on Broadway. Patty Duke and Anne Bancroft play Helen Keller and Annie Sullivan, respectively. Both go on to appear in the 1962 film as well.

| 1960 | The Student Non-Violent Coordinating Committee is founded to encourage voter registration among blacks in the southern United States. |

1962–1990 Nelson Mandela is jailed in South Africa for protesting apartheid. During his imprisonment, his wife, Winnie, continues to devote herself to the antiapartheid movement.

1963 Fannie Lou Hamer is arrested on the way home from a civil rights meeting and beaten while in jail.

1964–1975 War in Vietnam. The United States enters the conflict as the military ally of South Vietnam, battling Communist forces in the North.

1967 The National Organization for Women (NOW) holds its first meeting in Washington, D.C., where it adopts a Bill of Rights.

1970 Maggie Kuhn initiates her crusade for the rights of retired Americans.

1972 The United States Congress passes the Equal Employment Act, which provides for preferential hiring and promotions to women and minorities.

American anti-feminist Phyllis Schlafly founds the Stop ERA Foundation to oppose passage of the Equal Rights Amendment.

1973 The National Black Feminist Organization is established to address the double problem of racism and sexism.

The United States Supreme Court rules in favor of attorney Sarah Weddington in her case *Roe v. Wade*. For the first time abortion is legal in America.

1975 Boycotts led by Dolores Huerta persuade the United States Congress to pass the Agricultural Labor Relations Act, granting migrant workers bargaining rights.

1976 Mairead Corrigan-Maguire and Betty Williams receive the Nobel Peace Prize for their campaign to bring peace to Northern Ireland.

1979 The United States mint issues a new silver dollar coin with a portrait of Susan B. Anthony on it.

Angela Davis

1980 American feminist, activist, and educator Angela Davis runs for vice-president of the United States as a member of the Communist party. Neither this campaign nor a second one in 1984 are successful, but they attract public attention to her cause.

1983 Marian Edelman's Children's Defense Fund launches a major campaign to prevent teen pregnancy, an increasing problem in the United States.

1989 The Cold War ends. In Germany, the Berlin Wall is demolished, and the country is reunited.

In Beijing's Tiananmen Square, Chinese students stage demonstrations to demand greater democracy. They are ruthlessly shot down by the government forces.

1992 Native American women leaders from 20 tribes meet for the 4th annual Conference of Female Chiefs.

1997 Within less than a week, the lives of two of the world's most beloved humanitarians end. Princess Diana is killed in a car accident in Paris on August 31st. Mother Teresa dies in Calcutta on September 5th.

GLOSSARY

Abolition: literally, the act of getting rid of something. In American history the word is used most often to mean ending slavery.

Activist: a person who believes that the way to effect social or political reform is to take direct, decisive action when confronted with controversial issues.

Amendment: literally, correction. An amendment to a state or local constitution either changes the existing law or provides clarification of a legal issue that was not addressed before.

Anarchist: a person who rebels against any established authority and believes that people should be allowed to govern themselves. The word "anarchy" is often used in a derogatory sense, to indicate complete disorder or chaos.

Atheist: a person whose system of beliefs is based on the idea that there is no Supreme being.

Bar: in legal terms, the bar is the same as the court. A lawyer must pass a qualifying examination to be allowed to participate in court procedures.

Boycott: to refuse to deal with a person or organization whose policies are unjust or unacceptable. The word comes from Charles Boycott, an Irish landlord who lived during the late 19th century. He was shunned by his community for demanding excessively high rents from his tenants.

Canonization: the formal act by the Christian church of declaring a person a saint.

Capitalist: a person who upholds an economic system in which private individuals or corporations own the means of production and collect profits from them.

Caste: in Hinduism, a social class that is determined by birth. Although no longer as strictly enforced as they used to be, traditionally the castes are ranked from highest to lowest, and people are only allowed to pursue occupations specific to their class.

Censorship: the practice of officially controlling opinions and ideas expressed in printed works, radio, or by the visual media, apparently for the purpose of protecting the society.

Dissertation: an extended argument or explanation of a topic, presented either in writing or (less commonly) as a speech. The term is used most often to indicate the written work that graduate students must successfully complete before receiving a Ph.D.

Feminist: a person who believes that women should be socially, politically, and economically equal to men.

Guerrilla: from the Spanish word meaning "little war." A guerrilla is a person who acts alone or as part of a small group to fight a political enemy. Guerrillas are known for using acts of terrorism and sabotage to advance their cause. Sometimes independent rebel groups engage in guerrilla tactics, but a country's traditional military force might also authorize such actions as part of a larger campaign.

Home rule: a system in which a colony is governed by its local inhabitants, while still remaining under the control of the nation that has conquered the land.

Humanitarian: a person who seeks to promote the welfare of humanity.

Hunger strike: a protest in which participants refuse to eat until their demands are met.

Jim Crow laws: in the popular musical theater entertainments of 19th-century America, Jim Crow was a generic name for a stereotyped black man. Jim Crow laws enforced racial segregation.

Liberal: like the word "liberty," liberal comes from the Latin *libertas*, or freedom. In politics, a liberal is a person who believes in the free rights of the individual and seeks to protect and promote them through legislation.

Martyr: a person who submits to death or terrible suffering rather than betray her or his strongly held principles or beliefs, often of a religious nature.

Militant: aggressively engaged in promoting a cause, often to the point of being willing to participate in violent acts.

Missionary: a person whose purpose—or "mission"—is to convert people to the Christian religion.

Ordain: to formally invest a person with the office of a priest, minister, or rabbi.

Pacifism: the belief that violence is never justified as a way of settling conflicts.

Petition: a document submitted to an official body, usually a government, formally requesting changes in laws or policies.

Ph.D.: an abbreviation of the Latin term *philosophiae doctor*, or "doctor of philosophy." A Ph.D. is an advanced graduate degree that is awarded upon completion of a specialized program of academic study in the liberal arts or sciences.

Philanthropist: a humanitarian. The term is most often used to describe people who have the financial means to dedicate large sums of money to the charitable causes they support.

Political prisoner: a person who is imprisoned for holding unpopular or "threatening" political beliefs, even though he or she may not have committed a crime.

Radical: extreme as opposed to traditional or cautious.

Segregation: the process of keeping groups separate from one another, most often used in the sense of discrimination against races or classes.

Settlement house: a communal institution that provides a wide range of social services, and where social workers live among the people who have come to them for help.

Sit-in: a nonviolent form of protest in which the participants gather in a set location and remain there until their demands are heard. The term comes from the time of the American Civil Rights movement, when African American activists would occupy seats in segregated establishments and refuse to leave them for the duration of the protest.

Strike: to refuse to work until an employer agrees to certain demands.

Suffrage: the right to vote; also, the act of exercising that right.

Temperance: literally, the word "temperance" means moderation. Among the 19th-century reformers, however, it was defined as complete abstinence from alcoholic beverages.

Terrorist: a person who makes use of extreme violence in an attempt to force people to meet his or her political demands.

Triumvir: one member of a triumvirate, a ruling commission that is made up of three people (the word *triumvirate* comes from the Latin for "three men"). At the time of Hortensia, the triumvirate that ruled ancient Rome was made up of Mark Antony, Octavian, and Lepidus.

Union or labor union: an organization dedicated to protecting and promoting the rights of laborers.

Workers' compensation: a social welfare program that has been adopted in some form throughout most of the world. Workers' compensation laws require employers to provide certain financial compensation to workers if they are injured on the job or if they contract job-related illnesses.

INDEX

Numbers in boldface type indicate main entries.

CREDITS

Quotes

8 Addams, Jane. *Newer Ideals of Peace*. New York: The Macmillan Company, 1907. **11** Bambara, Toni Cade. From a lecture delivered at Livingston College, Rutgers University. Used by permission. **22** Ch'iu Chin. From Linthwaite, Illona, editor. *Ain't I a Woman! A Book of Woman's Poetry from Around the World*. New York: Peter Bedrick Books, 1988. By permission of NTC Publishing Group. **30** Edelman, Marian. *The Measure of Our Success*. Boston: Beacon Press, 1992. Used by permission. **33** Goldman, Emma. *Anarchism and Other Essays*. New York: Dover Publications, 1969. **39** Hutchinson, Anne. From Adams, Charles Francis, editor. *Antinomianism in the Colony of Massachusetts Bay, 1636–1638*. Boston: The Prince Society, 1894. **49** Menchú, Rigoberta. *I Rigoberta Menchú: An Indian Woman in Guatemala*. Edited and introduced by Elisabeth Burgos-Debray, translated by Ann Wright. Translation © 1984 by Verso. Used by permission of Verso Editions. **53** Nightingale, Florence. *Notes on Nursing: What It Is, and What It Is Not*. London: Harrison and Sons, 1860. **57** Priesand, Sally. *Judaism and the New Woman*. New York: Behrman House, Inc., 1975. Used by permission of Sally Priesand. **63** Stone, Lucy. From Wheeler, Leslie, editor. *Loving Warriors: Selected Letters of Lucy Stone and Henry B. Blackwell, 1853–1893*. New York: The Dial Press, 1981.

Photographs

Abbreviations

AP   AP Wide World Photos
COR   Corbis
HG   Hulton Getty
LOC   Library of Congress
NPG   National Portrait Gallery, Smithsonian Institute

Pages: 8 Adamson, Joy, HG. **9 (and title page)** Anthony, Susan B., LOC. **10 (and 7)** Baker, Ella, LOC. **11** Balch, Emily, LOC. **12** Beaufort, Margaret, LOC. **13** Bethune, Mary McLeod, LOC. **14** Blackwell, Alice, LOC. **15** Blatch, Harriot, LOC. **17** Booth, Maud, LOC; Boupacha, Djamila, LOC. **19** Butler, Josephine, LOC. **20** Cabrini, Frances Xavier, LOC; Castellanos, Rosario, photography by Ricardo Salazar, LOC. **21** Catt, Carrie Chapman, LOC. **23** Cobbe, Frances, HG; Cole, Johnnetta, photography by Annemarie Poyo, courtesy of Emory University. **24** Corrigan-Maguire, Mairead, HG. **25** Cunard, Nancy, LOC; Daly, Mary, photography by Gail Bryan, courtesy of Harper San Francisco. **27 (and cover)** Diana, Princess of Wales, AP. **28** Douglass, Anna Murray, LOC. **29** Eddy, Mary Baker, LOC. **30** Fawcett, Millicent Garrett, COR/Hulton-Deutsch Collection. **31** Flynn, Elizabeth Gurley, LOC. **32** Friedan, Betty, W. W. Norton & Co. **33 (and 7)** Gonne, Maude, LOC. **34** Greer, Germaine, HG. **35** Hamer, Mary Lou, LOC. **36 (and title page)** Height, Dorothy, LOC. **37** Hill, Octavia, HG. **38 (and cover)** Huerta, Dolores, courtesy of AFL-CIO. **39** Ireland, Patricia, courtesy of National Organization for Women. **40** Jackson, Helen, LOC. **41** Joan of Arc, LOC. **42** Jones, Mary, LOC. **44** King, Coretta, LOC. **45** Kollontay, Alexandra, LOC; Kuhn, Maggie, photography by Julie Jensen. **47** Low, Juliette, LOC. **47 (and title page)** Luxemburg, Rosa, LOC. **48** McPherson, Aimee Semple, LOC. **50 (and 6)** Montessori, Maria, LOC; Mott, Lucretia, NPG. **51** Naidu, Sarojini, LOC. **52** Nation, Carry, LOC. **53** Norman, Mildred, courtesy of Friends of the Peace Pilgrim. **54** Norton, Caroline, LOC. **55** Parks, Rosa, LOC. **56** Paul, Alice, LOC. **58** Sanger, Margaret, COR/Bettmann. **59** Schlafly, Phyllis, courtesy of the Eagle Forum. **60** Shabazz, Betty, COR/Bettmann. **61** Stanton, Elizabeth Cady, LOC. **62 (and cover)** Steinem, Gloria, LOC. **63** Stopes, Marie, LOC. **65 (and title page)** Mother Teresa, HG; **65** Truth, Sojourner, NPG. **67** Wald, Lillian, LOC. **69** Williams, Jody, AP. **70** Zetkin, Clara, HG. **72 (and cover)** Tubman, Harriet, LOC. **73 (and 6)** Pankhurst, Emmeline, LOC. **74** Salomon, Alice, LOC; Keller, Helen, LOC. **75** Davis, Angela, LOC.